First World War
and Army of Occupation
War Diary
France, Belgium and Germany

52 DIVISION
156 Infantry Brigade
Cameronians (Scottish Rifles)
7th Battalion
1 April 1918 - 31 March 1919

WO95/2897/4

The Naval & Military Press Ltd
www.nmarchive.com
Published in association with The National Archives

Published by

The Naval & Military Press Ltd

Unit 10 Ridgewood Industrial Park,

Uckfield, East Sussex,

TN22 5QE England

Tel: +44 (0) 1825 749494

www.naval-military-press.com

www.nmarchive.com

This diary has been reprinted in facsimile from the original. Any imperfections are inevitably reproduced and the quality may fall short of modern type and cartographic standards.

© Crown Copyright
Images reproduced by permission of The National Archives, London, England, 2015.

Contents

Document type	Place/Title	Date From	Date To
Heading	WO95/2897-4		
Heading	52nd Division 156th Infy Bde 1-7th Bn Scottish Rifles (Cameronians) Apr 1918-Mar 1919		
Heading	156th Brigade 52nd Division Disembarked Marseilles From Egypt 17.4.18 1/7th Battalion The Cameronians (Scottish Rifles) April 1918		
Miscellaneous	D.A.G 3rd Echelon	06/05/1918	06/05/1918
War Diary	Surafend	01/04/1918	03/04/1918
War Diary	Kantara	04/04/1918	04/04/1918
War Diary	Alexandria	05/04/1918	05/04/1918
War Diary	H.M.T. Leasowe Castle	05/04/1918	11/04/1918
War Diary	At Sea	12/04/1918	16/04/1918
War Diary	Marseilles	17/04/1918	18/04/1918
War Diary	Troop Train	18/04/1918	21/04/1918
War Diary	St. Firmin	21/04/1918	25/04/1918
War Diary	Rincq	26/04/1918	30/04/1918
Operation(al) Order(s)	Operation Order No. 12 by Major R. Blair Comdg 1/7th Bn The Cameronians (Scottish Rifles)	01/04/1918	01/04/1918
Operation(al) Order(s)	Operation Order No. 13 by Lieut Col J.G.P. Romanes D.S.O. Comdg 1/7th Bn The Cameronians (Scottish Rifles)	02/04/1918	02/04/1918
Miscellaneous	Appendix III Strength of 1/7th Cameronians as sailed from Egypt on 11th April, 1918.	11/04/1918	11/04/1918
Miscellaneous	List of Officers of 1/7th Cameronians Sailing from Egypt	11/04/1918	11/04/1918
Operation(al) Order(s)	Operation Order No. 14 by Lieut Col J.G.P. Romanes D.S.O. Comdg 1/7th Bn The Cameronians (Scottish Rifles)	17/04/1918	17/04/1918
Operation(al) Order(s)	Operation Order No. 15 by Lieut Col J.G.P. Romanes D.S.O. Comdg 1/7th Bn The Cameronians (Scottish Rifles)	24/04/1918	24/04/1918
Heading	War Diary For 1st To 31st May 1918 1/7th Bn. The Cameronians (Scottish Rifles) Volume XXXVI		
War Diary	Rincq	01/05/1918	08/05/1918
War Diary	Mont St Eloy.	09/05/1918	15/05/1918
War Diary	Trenches	16/05/1918	24/05/1918
War Diary	Reserve Trenches	25/05/1918	31/05/1918
Miscellaneous	Regimental Exercise		
Miscellaneous	Special Idea		
Miscellaneous	Task I		
Operation(al) Order(s)	Operation Order No. 16 by Lieut Col J.G.P. Romanes D.S.O. Comdg 1/7th Bn The Cameronians (Scottish Rifles)	06/05/1918	06/05/1918
Operation(al) Order(s)	Operation Order No. 17 by Lieut Col J.G.P. Romanes D.S.O. Comdg 1/7th Bn The Cameronians (Scottish Rifles)	06/05/1918	06/05/1918
Miscellaneous	Training Programme		
Operation(al) Order(s)	Operation Order No. 18 by Lieut Col J.G.P. Romanes D.S.O. Comdg 1/7th Bn The Cameronians (Scottish Rifles)	13/05/1918	13/05/1918

Miscellaneous	Trench Standing Orders		
Map	Extract From Map Of Mardeuil		
Heading	War Diary For June 1918 1/7th Battn The Cameronians (Scottish Rifles) Volume XXXVII		
Miscellaneous	Strength With Lest		
War Diary	Reserve Trenches (Thelus)	01/06/1918	02/06/1918
War Diary	Mont St Eloy	03/06/1918	11/06/1918
War Diary	Front Line Trenches	12/06/1918	19/06/1918
War Diary	Reserve Trenches	20/06/1918	29/06/1918
War Diary	Mont St Eloi	29/06/1918	30/06/1918
Map	Map		
Miscellaneous	Appendix II Lt Col. J.G.P. Romanes. D.S.O. Commanding 1/7th Cameronians (Scottish Rifles) 1st June 1918.	01/06/1918	01/06/1918
Miscellaneous	Programme Of Training	28/06/1918	28/06/1918
Map	Toast Area Vimy Ridge		
Operation(al) Order(s)	Operation Order No. 20 by Lieut Col J.G.P. Romanes D.S.O. Comdg 1/7th Bn The Cameronians (Scottish Rifles)	07/06/1918	07/06/1918
Operation(al) Order(s)	Operation Order No. 21 by Lieut Col J.G.P. Romanes D.S.O. Comdg 1/7th Bn The Cameronians (Scottish Rifles)	08/06/1918	08/06/1918
Miscellaneous	Appendix V 7th The Cameronians Patrols-11-6-18 to 20-6-18. Reference Maroeuil. 1/20,000.	20/06/1918	20/06/1918
Map	Support Battalion		
Heading	1/7th Cameronians (S.R.) War Diary For July 1918 Vol 4		
War Diary	Mont St Eloy	01/07/1918	07/07/1918
War Diary	Willerval Sector	08/07/1918	15/07/1918
War Diary	Brown Line Vimy	16/07/1918	21/07/1918
War Diary	Mont St. Eloy	22/07/1918	22/07/1918
War Diary	Bois d'Olhain	23/07/1918	29/07/1918
War Diary	Ecoivres	30/07/1918	31/07/1918
Miscellaneous	Strength In The Field	30/06/1918	30/06/1918
Miscellaneous	Training Programme		
Miscellaneous	Operations Orders By Capt W. Mather Comdg 1/7th Bn The Cameronians (Sco Rifles)	06/07/1918	06/07/1918
Operation(al) Order(s)	156th Infantry Brigade Order No. 42	05/07/1918	05/07/1918
Miscellaneous	158th Infantry Brigade Order No. 48	06/07/1918	06/07/1918
Miscellaneous	158th Infantry Brigade Administrative Order No. 6	06/07/1918	06/07/1918
Map	Map		
Miscellaneous	Operation Order Lieut Col J.G.P. Romanes D.S.O. Cmdg 1/7th Cameronians (Scottish Rifles)	14/07/1918	14/07/1918
Map	Map		
Miscellaneous	Provisional Battalion	20/07/1918	20/07/1918
Miscellaneous	Operation Orders Lieut Col J.G.P. Romanes D.S.O. Cmdg Bn The Cameronians (Sco Rifles)	21/07/1918	21/07/1918
Miscellaneous	Training Programme	25/07/1918	25/07/1918
Miscellaneous	Operation Orders Lieut Col J.G.P. Romanes D.S.O. Cmdg Bn the Cameronians (Sco Rifles)	29/07/1918	29/07/1918
Heading	1/7th Cameronians (S.R.) War Diary For August 1918 Volume XXXIX		
War Diary	Gavrelle	01/08/1918	15/08/1918
War Diary	Savy	16/08/1918	20/08/1918
War Diary	Warlus	21/08/1918	22/08/1918
War Diary	In The Field	22/08/1918	31/08/1918

Miscellaneous	Strength In The Field	31/07/1918	31/07/1918
Map	Disposition Sketch		
Miscellaneous	Operation Orders Lieut Col J.G.P. Romanes D.S.O. Cmdg Cameronians (Sco Rifles)	05/08/1918	05/08/1918
Map	Disposition Sketch		
Miscellaneous	Operations Orders By Lieut Col J.G.P. Romance D.S.O. Comdg Bn The Cameronians (Sco Rifles)	15/08/1918	15/08/1918
Miscellaneous	Operations Orders By Lieut Col J.G.P. Romance D.S.O. Comdg Bn The Cameronians (Sco Rifles)	31/08/1918	31/08/1918
Heading	1/7th Cameronians (Scottish Rifles) September 1918 Vol 40		
War Diary	T 24 D 75	01/09/1918	02/09/1918
War Diary	U 30 D	03/09/1918	06/09/1918
War Diary	B 2 D 2 7	07/09/1918	23/09/1918
War Diary	D17a 8.5.	23/09/1918	25/09/1918
War Diary	L 3.C.6.6	27/09/1918	27/09/1918
War Diary	L 3. C	28/09/1918	29/09/1918
War Diary	L 3.C.6.6	27/09/1918	30/09/1918
Miscellaneous	Strength In The Field	30/08/1918	30/08/1918
Heading	War Diary Of 1/7th Cameronians (S.R.) 1st To 31st October 1918 Volume XVI		
War Diary	L.3.C.	01/10/1918	07/10/1918
War Diary	Penin	07/10/1918	26/10/1918
War Diary	Lecelles	27/10/1918	30/10/1918
War Diary	Mont Du Proy	30/10/1918	31/10/1918
Miscellaneous	Strength In The Field	30/09/1918	30/09/1918
Heading	War Diary 7th Bn The Cameronians (Scottish Rifles) November 1918 Volume XLII		
War Diary	Mont Du Proy	01/11/1918	01/11/1918
War Diary	Mairie De Nivelle	01/11/1918	08/11/1918
War Diary	Hergnies	09/11/1918	09/11/1918
War Diary	Blaton	09/11/1918	10/11/1918
War Diary	Sirault	10/11/1918	10/11/1918
War Diary	Herchies	10/11/1918	10/11/1918
War Diary	Erbaut	11/11/1918	11/11/1918
War Diary	Herchies	12/11/1918	26/11/1918
War Diary	Lens Refce Toupnai 1/100000	27/11/1918	30/11/1918
War Diary	Lens	30/11/1918	30/11/1918
Miscellaneous	Strength In The Field		
Miscellaneous	Operation Orders by Captain D.R. Nelson M.C. Cmdg 1/7th Cameronians (Sco Rif)	01/11/1918	01/11/1918
Miscellaneous	Operation Orders by Captain D.R. Nelson M.C. Cmdg 1/7 Bn Cameronians (Sco Rif)	02/11/1918	02/11/1918
Miscellaneous	Operation Orders by Captain D.R. Nelson M.C. Cmdg 1/7 Bn Cameronians (Sco Rifles)	05/11/1918	05/11/1918
Miscellaneous	Provisional Operation Orders by Captain D.P. Nelson M.C. Comdg 1/7th Cameronians (Sco. Rifles)	05/11/1918	05/11/1918
Miscellaneous	Operation Orders by Captain D.R. Nelson M.C. Cmdg 1/7th Cameronians (Sco Rifles)	08/11/1918	08/11/1918
Miscellaneous	Operation Orders	10/11/1918	10/11/1918
Operation(al) Order(s)	Operation Orders No. X By Lieut Col J.G.P. Romanes D.S.O. Comdg 1/7th Cameronians (Sco Rifles)	26/11/1918	26/11/1918
Operation(al) Order(s)	Operation Orders No. Y By Lieut Col J.G.P. Romanes D.S.O. Comdg 1/7th Cameronians (Scottish Rifles)	28/11/1918	28/11/1918
Heading	War Diary 7th Bn The Cameronians (Scottish Rifles) December 1918 Volume XLIII		

War Diary	Lens	01/12/1918	31/12/1918
Miscellaneous	Strength in the Field	31/12/1918	31/12/1918
Heading	War Diary 7th Bn The Cameronians (Scottish Rifles) January 1919 Volume XLIV		
War Diary	Lens	01/01/1919	31/01/1919
Heading	War Diary 1/7th Cameronians (Scottish Rifles) March 1919		
War Diary	Lens Belgium	01/03/1919	16/03/1919
War Diary	Lens Belgium Soignies	17/03/1919	31/03/1919
Miscellaneous	Strength in the Field	31/01/1919	31/01/1919

WD 917/2297 (4)

WD 917/2297 (4)

52ND DIVISION
156TH INFY BDE

1-7TH BN SCOTTISH RIFLES
(CAMERONIANS)
APR 1918-MAR 1919

156th Brigade
52nd Division.

Disembarked MARSEILLES from EGYPT 17.4.18.

1/7th BATTALION

THE CAMERONIANS (Scottish Rifles)

APRIL 1918.

To: DAG
    3rd Echelon,
    G.H.Q.
    B.E.F.

Secret.   S.R.G. 94

Herewith enclosed War Diary of this Unit for April 1918, please.

E.S. Romanes
Lieut Colonel
Comdg. 17th Cameronians
(Scottish Rifles)

6/5/18

Army Form C. 2118.

WAR DIARY
or
INTELLIGENCE SUMMARY. April 1918. A.(2).
(Erase heading not required.)

Instructions regarding War Diaries and Intelligence Summaries are contained in F. S. Regs., Part II. and the Staff Manual respectively. Title pages will be prepared in manuscript.

Place	Date	Hour	Summary of Events and Information	Remarks and references to Appendices
SURAFEND	1		The Brigade Sports were concluded and passed off successfully. A number of side-shows had been arranged and proved particularly attractive. Further orders were received from Brigade for entraining at LUDD on 3rd April. A Dump was formed at LUDD of all baggage and equipment that could be spared and the necessary for the remaining two days being retained.	(Appendix I)
SURAFEND	2		Lieut. Col. ROMANES, D.S.O. relinquished command of 156th Brigade on return of Brig-Gen LEGGETT D.S.O. from short leave, and resumed command of the Batln. During the afternoon all vehicles and animals of Regimental Transport were returned to Ordnance and Remount Depots respectively	
SURAFEND	3	0730	All surplus stores returned to Ordnance and remaining baggage despatched to station at LUDD.	(Appendix II)
		1200	Batn. paraded and marched to LUDD. On arrival entraining commenced and was completed by	

WAR DIARY

INTELLIGENCE SUMMARY.

(Erase heading not required.)

Army Form C. 2118.

(A)(3).

Place	Date	Hour	Summary of Events and Information	Remarks and references to Appendices
KANTARA	4	1415	Train moved off at 1500. The only stops of any length were at GAZA and EL ARISH. At GAZA dinner was provided for officers at the Refreshment tent.	MW
			Arrived KANTARA EAST at 0645. The Battalion detrained immediately and marched to No. 2 Infantry Base Depot where the day was spent. The following reinforcements joined from No. 1 Base Depot — Lieut. Arundell (from hospital) 2/Lt. A.O. Hillier (from hospital) 2/Lt Brooks (from hospital) 2/Lt R. Henshaw 2/Lt Sutton 2/Lt. (?) Hanks, and 82 O.R. (mostly transferred from A.S.C. and R.A.M.C.) 2/Lts Austin and Forbes, who had been sent on from SURAFEND in advance reported. Lt. Officers and O.R. who had been sent from SARONA to attend courses, also returned to the Bn. during the day. The strength in officers was made up to 37, being the maximum allowed, and a number of reinforcements held to be left behind at KANTARA. Draft of 6 2 Other ranks taken on Strength.	MW
		2130	Battn. Paraded and marched to KANTARA WEST where	MW

A5834 Wt W4973/M687 750,000 8/16 D.D. & L. Ltd. Forms/C.2118/13

WAR DIARY
INTELLIGENCE SUMMARY

Army Form C. 2118.

Place	Date	Hour	Summary of Events and Information	Remarks and references to Appendices
ALEXANDRIA	5.	0600	It snowed after some delay. The train left at 2400. Arrived GABBARY QUAY, ALEXANDRIA. The Bath. immediately entrained. The quay was crowded already by 1/4th Bn. The Royal Scots and 1/7th Bn. The Royal Scots. Both these Battalions had instructions to embark in the same ship as ourselves viz HMT. LEASOWE CASTLE and embarkation proceeded very ably. It was completed about 1200. (Details of embarkation etc. v. APPENDIX III) The Battalion is distributed on four troop decks and fairly crowded. Accommodation for officers is excellent. Brig. Gen. LEGGETT DSO. is in command of troops on board. Besides ourselves the following units are on board — 156th Brigade Staff, 1/4th Royal Scots, 1/7th Royal Scots, 1 Sect. of 1/1st Lowland Field Ambulance, 220th Coy. A.S.C.	
HMT. LEASOWE CASTLE	6	10.00	Inspection of Troop Decks by Commanding Officer. During the day Ship moved out into harbour but only a short distance from Quay.	
	7	0945	Parade at emergency stations for C.O.'s inspection. O.C. Troops held inspection at 1000. Men parades are to be held daily at the same hour.	

Army Form C. 2118.

WAR DIARY
INTELLIGENCE SUMMARY.
(Erase heading not required.)

April 1918.

Instructions regarding War Diaries and Intelligence Summaries are contained in F.S. Regs., Part II. and the Staff Manual respectively. Title pages will be prepared in manuscript.

Place	Date	Hour	Summary of Events and Information	Remarks and references to Appendices
H.M.T. LEASOWE CASTLE	7	1600	Practice alarm. Lifebelts were issued to all ranks on this parade and are at all times to be in possession of their owners.	
	8		Manual parade in the morning and practice alarm in the afternoon. Permission was given by GC troops to allow three officers per battalion ashore to Alexandria each day whilst the ship remains in harbour. Before dinner Brig-Gen LEGGETT, D.S.O. read to all officers letters from Gen. Sir H. ALLENBY and Lieut. Gen. Sir E. BULFIN to Major Gen. HILL commanding 52nd (LOWLAND) Division thanking him (Gen. HILL) and his Division for their work in the past and wishing them good fortune in the future.	
	9		Manual parades. Heard e.g. L. Morgan left for KANTARA to join R.F.C. There have been many complaints since coming on board regarding the men's meeting. The matter is being gradually rectified by the Ship's authorities but complaints are still present.	
	10	1400	During morning parade several lifeboats were lowered and men practised in manning them rapidly. After lunch left the ship in two lighters and proceeded to the breakwater for bathing - returning about 1600.	

Army Form C. 2118.

WAR DIARY
INTELLIGENCE SUMMARY.
(Erase heading not required.)

April, 1918.

A.(6).

Place	Date	Hour	Summary of Events and Information	Remarks and references to Appendices
H.M.T. LEASOWE CASTLE	11th	0820	Practice Alarm. 1000. Inspection and parades. Maj. Gen. HILL cmdg. 52nd Division is to sail on board this transport and came on board at 1030.	App.3.ft.
		1430.	The entire Convoy (7 transports, and escort of 6 destroyers and one cruiser) left ALEXANDRIA Harbour.	
At SEA	12th 13th 14th 15th 16th		Inspection daily at 1000. Occasional practice alarm parades. The voyage on the whole was pleasant, but uneventful.	
MARSEILLES	17th	0730	Arrived in MARSEILLES Harbour, and immediately docked. All other units disembarked during the day, this Battalion remaining on board overnight.	Appendix IV
	18th	0530	Disembarkation commenced, and completed by 0615. Entraining immediately commenced. This was completed in good time. The train was overcrowded.	
		0905	Left MARSEILLES. Reached LE TEIL 22.30, where hot water was provided for making tea, which was issued to the men.	App.3.ft.
TROOP TRAIN	19th		Reached PERCY LE MONCY about 12.15, where a hot meal was served, and tea again served.	
	20th		Everyone missing their hay just. Ghad meal at U.S., at midday, at 21.20. Reveilly Stealing of the horn going on...	App.5.ft.

MAP REFERENCE
ABBEVILLE 1/100,000

Army Form C. 2118.

WAR DIARY
or
INTELLIGENCE SUMMARY.
(Erase heading not required.)

A.17.

Place	Date APRIL	Hour	Summary of Events and Information	Remarks and references to Appendices
TROOPTRAIN.	21st	0130	Reached ABBEVILLE, where the train remained until 0520. Reached NOYELLES at 0630, and detrained. The journey had not been a very comfortable one for the men, owing to the rail tracks and much ex-perience. Instructions received for the Battalion to proceed to Hutels at St. FIRMIN. Advanced parties and baggage left by motor transport 0945. Batt also left NOYELLES at 1130, arriving at St. FIRMIN 1330. Billeting the Batt was a matter of considerable difficulty, as suitable accommodation was scarce.	
St. FIRMIN.		1030	The following officers, having joined from U.K., were posted for duty to Companies as under:—	
			"A" Coy. "B" Coy. "C" Coy. "D" Coy. 2/Lt. R.G. Leas. 2/Lt. Austin. Singer. 2/Lt. Aul. Boyd. 2/Lt. H.S. Thomson " J. Deacon. " G. Best. " Q.M. Quinn. " R.f.S. Smith. " H. Ross. " A. Gordon.	O. & S. Lt
	22nd		The day spent at short gas drill parades, and general cleaning up. Further transport drawn at ABBEVILLE.	A.&.S.Lt.
	23rd		Gas training. Musketry. Route march by companies.	A.&.S.Lt.
	24th		Training and route march. Instructions received for Batt- moving on 25th inst.	A.&.S.Lt.
	25th	14:30	The Batt, less "C"Coy, left St. FIRMIN, and marched to RUE, arriving at 15:30. Entraining immediately commenced.	Appendix V
		16:00	Train left RUE for WIZERNES.	A.&.S.Lt.

MAP REFERENCE.
HAZEBROUCK. 1/100,000 2nd Edn.

Army Form C. 2118.

WAR DIARY
or
INTELLIGENCE SUMMARY.
(Erase heading not required.)

A.(8).

Instructions regarding War Diaries and Intelligence Summaries are contained in F. S. Regs., Part II. and the Staff Manual respectively. Title pages will be prepared in manuscript.

Place	Date	Hour	Summary of Events and Information	Remarks and references to Appendices
	APRIL 1918.			
RINCQ.	26th	0400	Arrived at WIZERNES, and obtained billets arranged for there would not be occupied, but the Battn would proceed to REBECQ. (S.D.7.7).	
		1000	Batt. WIZERNES, awaiting at REBECQ at 1315, when further instructions were received to proceed to billets at RINCQ. (S.E.3.5), which was reached about 1400. Lieut. A.N. McLaurin appointed Batt. Scout Officer. 2/Lieut. A.D. Hillis, appointed Batt. Lewis Gun Officer.	A.8.5.ft.
	27th		To date 26-4-18. All containers of box respirators exchanged for new ones. Lecture on "Gas" to all officers by B.Gde G. Officers. Lieut. J.P. Smith to Batt. "A" Coy, as second in command. (via 9th M.Gunners).	A.8.5.ft. A.8.5.ft.
	28th		Being Sunday no parades were carried out.	
	29th		Training carried out in the morning. Bn. paraded and marched to Gas Area at S.D.9.7, and passed through the gas huts, (order test the Respirators). Returned 1630.	A.8.5.ft.
	30th	1300	Bn. paraded, and marched to training ground at S.D.6.7, to attend a lecture on Bayonet Fighting by Col. Campbell (Golden Hands.), which proved very interesting.	
		1500	Usual Training in the afternoon.	

J.A. Romney Lt Col

Army Form C. 2118.

WAR DIARY
or
INTELLIGENCE SUMMARY.
(Erase heading not required.)

APRIL 1918.

5th The Camerons.

	Officers.	Other ranks.
Strength in the Field { 1st April	24	740
{ 30th April	47	842
Increase	13	102

Total Increase - all ranks — 115

The month has been an eventful one in the history of the Battalion. After having been three years in the East, it has been at very short notice, transferred to the Western Front. In spite of the change of climate, which was keenly felt, the health of the Battalion has been good since landing in France.

Operation Order No: 12
by
Major R. Blair
Comdg. 1/7th Bn. The Cameronians (Scottish Rifles)

APPENDIX I

1st April 1918.

1. **Move.** The Battalion will be prepared to entrain at LUDD at 0800 on 3rd inst.

   All surplus Officers Kits will be sent off today and dumped near Station.

   One blanket per man and one bivouac sheet per man will be returned to Ordnance today. Waterproof sheets and S.B. Respirators at the scale of one per man will be drawn and issued.

   All tents will be handed into Q.M. Store by 1000 on 2nd inst.

2. **Rations.** Every man on arrival at LUDD will be complete with two days rations. Every man will have a full water bottle on entraining.

3. **Loading Parties.** One platoon per Coy. under an Officer will be detailed as loading parties. Lieut. McLaurin will be in charge of the whole party. This loading party will not be dismissed until embarkation is complete. O.C. Loading Party will ensure that a guard is placed on each wagon when loaded which will remain on duty until wagon is unloaded.

4. **Base Kits.** Base kits will be collected from Base Depot at KANTARA and proceed with Unit.

1 Copy to A Coy.
1 " " B "
1 " " C "
1 " " D "
1 " " Q.M.
1 " " Transport Officer
2 " " Diary

Capt & Adjutant
1/7th Cameronians
(Sco. Rifles)

Operation Order No. 13
by
Lieut. Col. [?] Romanis D.S.O.
Comdg. 1/7th Bn. Cameronians (Scottish Rifles)

APPENDIX II

2nd April 1918.

1. **Move.**   The Battalion will be paraded ready to move off at 1200 tomorrow. Order of march:- Bn. H.Q., A, B, C and D Coys.
      Loading party under Lieut. McLaurin will parade at 0930 at Bn. H.Q. and will proceed thence to LUDD Station.

2. **Transport.**   All Officers kits, mess stores and cookhouse material will be loaded on camels ready to move off with loading party at 0930. Sufficient dixies will be retained for midday meal. Lieut. McLaurin will see that his party has sufficient dixies wherewith to cook midday meal at LUDD.

3. **Bivouac Sheets.**   All bivouac sheets will be returned to Q.M. Store by 0700 tomorrow.

4. **Dress.**   Full marching order, greatcoat and blanket to be carried on the man.

5. **Detraining.**   The utmost expedition is to be observed in detraining at KANTARA. O.C. Coys. will arrange to have all men wakened at 0600 when packs will be made up and all preparations made for detraining.
      Lieut. McLaurin will ensure that there is no delay in unloading baggage.

1 Copy to A Coy.
1   "   B "
1   "   C "
1   "   D "
1   "   Q.M.
1   "   T.O.
2   "   Diary.

Harold C. Maclean
Capt. & Adjutant
1/7th Cameronians
(Sco. Rifles)

APPENDIX III

Strength of 1/7th Cameronians, as sailed from Egypt on 11th April, 1918.

	Officers	O.R.	Total
Battn. H.Q. (Including Transport)	11	165	176
"A" Coy.	6	176	182
"B" "	6	175	181
"C" "	6	182	188
"D" "	7	169	176
	36	867	903

APPENDIX III.

List of Officers of 1/7th Cameronians
sailing from Egypt on 11th April, 1918.

Battalion H.Q.

Lieut. Col. J. G. L. Romanes D.S.O.
Major R. Blair
Capt. & Adjt. H. C. Maclean M.C.
Capt. L. S. Gray
Hon. Capt. & Q.M. J. Phillips.
Lieut. G. Kerr
  " J. Austin
  " A. E. Bird M.C.
  " A. T. Coltart M.C.

Attached Capt. T. T. Apsimon, R.A.M.C.
  " J. R. Spence, C.F.

"A" Coy.

Capt. W. S. Bow
Lieut. A. N. McLaurin
2nd " C. Gillies
  " W. R. Burns
  " G. Brooks
  " A. J. Hood

"B" Coy.

Capt. D. R. Nelson
  " W. S. B. Wilson
Lieut. R. Barr
  " H. J. Forbes
2nd " W. T. Anderson
  " A. D. Hillier

"C" Coy.

Capt. L. C. S. Aitken
Lieut. C. Carmichael
2nd " J. W. Strathearn
  " D. Renton
  " F. Chrystal
  " S. Cullen

"D" Coy.

Capt. W. Mather
Lieut. A. Dunlop
  " J. D. Smith
2nd " D. McWilliam M.C.
  " H. Gourlay
  " D. McA. Reid
  " A. McGlashan

APPENDIX IV

Operation Order No 14
by
Lieut Col. G. S. Romanes D.S.O.
Comdg. 1/7th Bn. The Cameronians (Scottish Rifles)

17th April 1918.

1. Disembarkation. Battn. will disembark tomorrow as per following time-table.

"D" Coy. - 0500.
"A" " - 0515.
Battn. H.Q. - 0530.
"B" Coy. - 0545.
"C" " - 0600.

Having disembarked Coys. will proceed to railway siding - which will be pointed out - and prepare to entrain.

2. Baggage. All officers baggage will be dumped in Battn. dump on quay by 0530.

O.C. "D" Coy. will arrange on arriving at siding to dump packs and pile arms and send his Coy. back to Battn. dump to load kits and stores on motor lorries and carry balance to train.

O.C. "D" Coy. will ensure that his Coy. is at Battn. dump ready for work by 0550.

O.C. "B" Coy. will arrange to unload baggage from motor lorries at siding and to load it on train. Full particulars will be given on the spot.

3. Cleanliness. All decks must be left scrupulously clean and tidy.

1 Copy to "A" Coy.
1 " " B "
1 " " C "
1 " " D "
1 " " Q.M.
1 " " I.O.
2 " Diary.

Capt & Adjt.
1/7th Cameronians
(Sco. Rifles)

Operation Order
No 15. **APPENDIX V**
by
Lieut Col J.G.P. Romanes. D.S.O.
Comdg 1/7th The Cameronians (Scottish Rifles).

24th April. 1918.

1. **Move.** The Battn will move by rail to WIZERNES, leaving RUE Station at 1700 to-morrow.
Coys will form up in column of route on main road, head of the column ready to pass starting point at LES MORETTES FARM at 1445.
Order of march. HQ. A. B. D Coys.

2. **Advance Party.** The advance party, consisting of 1 officer per coy, will report to Lieut Austin at Bn HQ. at 0700. They will be mounted on bicycles, which they will obtain from QM. and will carry 24 hours rations.

3. **Water Carts.** Water carts will travel full.

4. **Rations** Meat ration will be carried in cookers, remainder on men.

5. **Transport.** Water proof sheets and 2nd blanket will be rolled in bundles of 10 and dumped at Q.M. Stores by 0800, limbers will be available for carriage.
Officers kit & mess stores will also be dumped at Q.M. Stores by 1300.

6. **Lewis Guns.** One limber per Coy will be available for L Gs.
These limbers will also carry 9 boxes S.A.A., which will be loaded at RUE Station.

7. **Signalling Stores**. Transport Officer will supply one limber for signalling Stores, Orderly Room Stores, and the four L. Guns of Bn H.Q.

8. **Cleanliness**. All billets, and billeting areas will be left scrupulously clean.

9. **Transport**. Transport Officer will arrange to have all vehicles and baggage (except as detailed below), at Station by 1400.

   O.C. B Coy will arrange to have a loading party of 1 Officer and 60 other ranks at Station at 1400. The Officer in charge of this party will report to Capt Cray, and receive further orders from him.

10. **Company Detached**. "C" Coy will not proceed with the Battn but will receive separate orders. Transport Officer will arrange to leave for their use one cooker and team.

(Sgd) Hector. C. McLean
Capt & Adjt.
1/7th The Cameronians.
(Sco Rif's).

Army Form C. 2118.

WAR DIARY
or
INTELLIGENCE SUMMARY.
(Erase heading not required.)

Original

WAR DIARY No. 2
for
1st to 31st MAY, 1918

17th Bn. The Cameronians (Scottish Rifles)

VOLUME XXXVI

WAR DIARY or INTELLIGENCE SUMMARY.

Army Form C. 2118.

MAP REFERENCE.
Sheet 36 c/40,000.

Place	Date May 1916	Hour	Summary of Events and Information	Remarks and references to Appendices
RINCQ	1st		Training. Inspection of clothing by Commanding Officer. Report as worn from 0930 to 1015 by everyone, however employed. This is now a standing order.	O.8.3. ft.
	2nd		Training. Lewis Guns (A + B Coys) carried out firing practice on No 4. 30 yds ranges at H.15.b.4.1. Lecture on Gas by Bde Gas Officer.	O.8.3. ft.
	3rd		Training. Range practice carried out by "C" + "D" Coys on ranges 9 and 10. (H.7.a.) Two lectures in the Town Hall AIRE, in the afternoon, on "Recent Operations". Three officers from Coy attended. Field Marshal Sir DOUGLAS HAIG, arrived during the course of his lecture, addressed the officers present and wished the Division good luck. 2 Lt G.W.B. Swayne, and 18 other ranks to Bde. L.T.M. Battery.	O.8.3. ft.
	4th	0900	Battalion paraded, and proceeded to Cran Cren, MAMETZ, for a demonstration in Smoke Helmets, Gas Respiration. Capt A.S. Niese, having reported for duty, was posted to Letter "C" Coy, and temporarily attached to H.Q.	O.8.3. ft.
	5th		Battalion Church Parade, arranged for 1030, cancelled owing to heavy rain. Tactical scheme for all officers in the afternoon. *Instructions received that the Div= was moving. Advance party 10 officer 3 oranks (Lt Austin) proceeded to AIRE for further instructions.	*APPENDIX 1 O.8.3. ft.
	6th		Training as usual. O.C. Coys took N.C.Os over tactical scheme of 5th inst. Bathing in the afternoon. A + B Coys. Lt J.D. Smith to METRINGHEIM in charge & of party for musketry course.	O.8.3. ft.

MAP REFERENCE.
SHEET 36ᵃ 1/40,000
LENS 1/100,000

Army Form C. 2118.

WAR DIARY
or
INTELLIGENCE SUMMARY
(Erase heading not required.)

A(3).

Place	Date	Hour	Summary of Events and Information	Remarks and references to Appendices
RINCQ	MAY 7th		Training. All available baggage and stores, sent off in advance with Battalion Transport, which left at 11.30. Bathing carried out in the morning.	O.&R.S.R.
	8th		Battalion moved to AIRE Station by companies (Appendix II). There was considerable delay at the Station, and entraining did not commence until 16.10. Train left 19.00, reaching ACQ (LENS 3H.9.2) about 03.00. Detraining took place immediately, and Battalion proceeded to billets in huts at MONT St. ELOY. (S.I.2.2), as Divisional Reserve.	APPENDIX II
MONT St. ELOY	9th		By this move, the Division was transferred from the XI to the XVIII Corps. Information received that the Germans were expected to attack VIMY RIDGE on the night of 9/10th. Alarm stations allotted to platoons. Transport was hurried up, ready to move. An alternative area was chosen, to be occupied in the event of the huts being shelled. Routes to the various switches which might have to be manned, were reconnoitred. The night passed quietly. (Capt. N. S.B. Wilson and 1 other rank to 1st ARMY Infantry School, HARDELOT.	O.&O.S.R.
	10th		Training, according to programme issued. Preparations for a rapid move still held.	APPENDIX III
	11th		Training. Range practice, and Lewis Gun taking carried out on ranges in the vicinity of the camp.	O.&R.S.R. O.&R.S.R.

Army Form C. 2118.

WAR DIARY
or
INTELLIGENCE SUMMARY.
(Erase heading not required.)

Ref. 51c/49,600
36c/40,000

Attached Diaries from MAROEUIL 1/20,000   A(4)

Instructions regarding War Diaries and Intelligence Summaries are contained in F. S. Regs., Part II. and the Staff Manual respectively. Title pages will be prepared in manuscript.

Place	Date	Hour	Summary of Events and Information	Remarks and references to Appendices
MONT ST. ELOY.	MAY 12th		No training. Church parade 10.30 in Y.M.C.A hut in camp (Rev. J. Spencer CF) Training and range practices. Lecture by the Commanding Officer to Officers and NCOs on Section Organisation.	Q.8.5 ft.
	13th		Training. Address to Officers and N.Cos by Brig Gen. A.H. Leggat, on which the Bde was going to occupy. The advance parties to Officers of the Bn on Contact Aeroplanes. Lecture by officers of the Bn on Contact Aeroplanes.	C.8.c.3 ft.
	14th		Parties proceed to Right Sector of Brigade front.	C.8.5 ft.
	15th		Battalion took over right sub-sector extending from WESTERN ROAD in the north to 300 yards south of the junction of TIRED ALLEY with PLUMER'S EXTN. Line was taken over from 1/5th Bn. K.O.S.B. Lieut. Col. J.G.P. ROMANES, D.S.O. in command. Dispositions — Right: D.Coy — Left Centre: B Coy — Left: A Coy. "C" Coy in support and occupying the following posts viz. 9th On Platoon ready for dislodging DURHAM SUBURB, BARNSLEY and FOVANT POSTS. Batn. H.Q. in east of WILLERVAL. Relief completed by 9 p.m. Seventy-two Officers proceeded into the line with the Battn. and the remainder with surplus personnel formed tracing the nucleus under Major BLAIR in RISPIN CAMP, VILLERS AU BOIS. The transport and Qm Batty went into camp near BERTHONVAL FARM MAROEUIL from During the day aeroplanes were very active, and there was considerable artillery activity on both sides. The weather remained fine all day and night.	APPENDIX IV / V. See APP VI MAROEUIL 1/20,000

REF. SIS 1:40,000
36 1:40,000
Attached tracing from MAROEUIL 1:10,000 A(5)

Army Form C. 2118.

WAR DIARY
INTELLIGENCE SUMMARY.
(Erase heading not required.)

Instructions regarding War Diaries and Intelligence Summaries are contained in F. S. Regs., Part II. and the Staff Manual respectively. Title pages will be prepared in manuscript.

Place	Date	Hour	Summary of Events and Information	Remarks and references to Appendices
Trenches	May 1918 16		Quiet day with fine but hazy weather. Aerial and artillery activity as yesterday. During the evening put over 15 gas shells (Yellow Cross). 2/Lt R.S.L. SMITH was slightly gassed, also 18 other ranks.	
	17		One N.C.O. and 3 men patrolled No Man's Land but heard or saw nothing. Weather good with bright moonlight at night. D Coy shelled between 5pm and 6pm — casualties one man killed and one wounded.	
	18		At night 2/Lt A. GORDON and S.O.R. on patrol. Three enemy were seen on returning. Quiet day along our front. Patrol at night of 2/Lt A.W.B. SINGER and on return lay in wait for the enemy but saw nothing. SUBURB POST was heavily shelled and one N.C.O. was killed.	
	19		Enemy shelled front with trench mortar shells in the early morning. Aerial activity as usual — artillery on both sides two active. 2/Lt G. BROOKS and 2/Lt D. RENTON with two sections reconnoitred enemy's wire. Weather continued fine. One man wounded by shell fire during night.	
	20		2/Lt RENTON and 2 sections examined enemy wire and lay in wait for enemy patrols, but nothing was seen to heard.	
	21		Quiet day. Bright moonlight at night which hindered patrolling. 2/Lt GORDON and 2 sections lay in wait for enemy patrols but none were encountered.	

REF- ATTD TRACING for
MAROEUIL 1: 20000

Army Form C. 2118.

WAR DIARY
or
INTELLIGENCE SUMMARY.
(Erase heading not required.)

A 6

Place	Date MAY	Hour	Summary of Events and Information	Remarks and references to Appendices
Trenches	21	1 a.m.	2/Lt W.N. Boyd and 2 sections examined enemy's wire. It was also intended that they would enter enemy's trenches but owing to moonlight they were observed and event made no progress. During the night the Battalion on our right were bombarded with gas shells and to effect was slightly felt in our lines. We had no casualties.	JWW
	22		Quiet day with fine weather. 2/Lt A.J. HOOD and 2 sections took up position in no man's land but saw nothing of the enemy.	JWW
	23	1.0 a.m.	2/Lt D. REID and 2 section lay in wait in no man's land but saw nothing of the enemy. During the day the Battalion was relieved in the line by 14th Royal Scots and went into support. The dispositions were as follows (see tracing) Battalion H.Q. in caves at THELUS. A Company in FARBUS WOOD B Company in BROWN LINE EAST of WILLERVAL C Company (at disposal of O.C. 14th Royal Scots) 2 Platoons in TIRED ALLEY and two platoons in dugout at N.E. of WILLERVAL D Company — 2 Platoons in SPUR POST, 1 Platoon in TAPE POST and one Platoon with Battalion H.Q.	APPENDIX VI JWW
	24		The weather turned down. Nothing of importance happened.	JWW

REF ATTD TRACING.
MAROEUIL 1" 20,000

WAR DIARY

INTELLIGENCE SUMMARY.
(Erase heading not required.)

AD

Place	Date May	Hour	Summary of Events and Information	Remarks and references to Appendices
RESERVE TRENCHES	25		The weather improved and there was bright moonlight at night. A patrol of D Coy of Bn. HQ took over BORDER POST. The post was in a very bad state and required much work. Enemy shelled FARBUS WOOD. No casualties. 7/Lt REID Evacuated sick.	JMU
	26		Fine weather and a quiet day. Yellow cross gas shell "A" and "D" Coy area slightly affected. 4 men gassed.	JMU
	27		In view of a raid intended to take place as soon as the moon permitted, Lieut A.W.B. SINGER accompanied a patrol of 1/4th Royal Scots to locate enemy post. It was not located. Enemy shelled THELUS during the afternoon.	JMU
	28	11pm	Lieut SINGER again accompanied patrol of 1/4 Royal Scots (in command of raid). Patrol (enemy's wire) was found to be uncompleted. An enemy M.G. post was located next day but was shelling. Lieut SINGER took out a platoon to suffer M.G. post discovered on previous night but found it unoccupied. Patrol examined enemy wire. The day passed quietly. There was again a good shelling into casualty.	JMU
	29	11:30pm	Raiding party under Lieut R. BARR with 2/Lt SINGER and 2/Lt GORDON with two platoons left on lines, unfortunately a party of 1/4 Royal Scots sent out as our covering party was discovered	JMU

REF. ATTACHED TRACING
MAROEUIL 1:79,000

Army Form C. 2118.

WAR DIARY
INTELLIGENCE SUMMARY
(Erase heading not required)

A8

Place	Date	Hour	Summary of Events and Information	Remarks and references to Appendices
RESERVE TRENCHES	May 1918			
	29		and the enemy threw M.G fire and put up flares. Subsequently, the enemy continuing his flares observed our party close to his wire and opened fire with machine guns from party. It was impossible to reach enemy lines and our party withdrew. We had 3 men wounded.	AW
	30		A quiet day with fine weather. In the evening a successful S.O.S. was carried out by our division.	GW
	31		Weather again fine. In the afternoon the Battalion Aid Post was shelled and one man killed. Enemy artillery was quiet.	GW

R.Blair Major
Comdg 1/7th Cameronians (Scottish Rifles)

Army Form C. 2118.

WAR DIARY
or
INTELLIGENCE SUMMARY.
(Erase heading not required.)

Instructions regarding War Diaries and Intelligence Summaries are contained in F. S. Regs., Part II. and the Staff Manual respectively. Title pages will be prepared in manuscript.

Place	Date	Hour	Summary of Events and Information	Remarks and references to Appendices

Strength of unit as at 30th April 1918
Strength of unit as at 31st May 1918

	Off.	O.R.
	46	830
	32	682

Alterations in Strength during month.

Increases
	Off.	O.R.
Reinforcements	1	95
From Hospital	—	69
From detachment and other causes	—	6
Total	1	100

Officers — Increase
Capt A.S. Price

Decreases
	Off.	O.R.
Killed	—	2
Wounded	—	11
Do (Gas)	1	74
Missing	1	7
To hospital (sick)	1	91
To Corps	4	19
On leave	5	80
Other	4	19
Total	15	248

Officers — Decrease
Lt. R.A.L. Smith (wounded S.W.)
Lt. D. Rea Rai (sick to hospital)
Capt R.C.A. Arthur
Capt W.S.B. Wilson } Corps
Lt. A.J. Biza
Lt. H.W. Forbes
Capt Lau Phillips
Lt. Allen
Lt. Pyrke } leave
Lt. Boga
Lt. Renton
Lt. Anderson W.T.
Capt A.P. Neal
Lt. Smiley
Lt. Boga
Lt. Scott

APPENDIX I

Regimental Exercise.

Sunday, May 5th.

1530.
Rendezvous – Railway bridge in H.26.b.
Officers only. Company Syndicates to be found for solutions.

Note.
Company Commanders to repeat the exercises with their N.C.O.s on subsequent afternoons. – C.O.'s solution to be accepted.

Regimental Exercise
Ref 1:40,000 Sheet 36.a

General Idea

On April 30th the Germans resumed the offensive and directed an overwhelming attack whose centre was on HINGES, and by 1800 on X day had forced our troops back on to the line —

[BETHUNE] - BURBURE - (U.27) - ST HILAIRE - (T.5) - QUERNES - (N.13) - AIRE - and the line of the canal de la LYS.

Of this line 156th Bde were holding from WITTERNESSE exclusive to N.3a.1.9.

During Y day desperate fighting took place all along the line, especially North of the canal D'AIRE. At 1600 our line ran AIRE - H.23.c.10.0 - along the canal - H.17. central - H.18. central - I.13 central - I.21.a. AIRE had been penetrated and the situation here at 1800 was most critical.

The Bde line had also been forced back to BLESSY - high ground in rear of St QUENTIN, though the latter was still occupied by our advanced troops.

Special Idea.

At 1800 orders are received to withdraw the line as follows after dark.

- K.Y Bde — BLESSY — G.35.a.9.9.
- 7th R.S. — G.35.a.9.9 — G.30.d.10.9.
- 7th S.R. — Along line of LYS River to Railway bridge H.26.b exclusive.
- 4th RS — Bridge inclusive — MOULIN LE COMPTE inclusive, with 157th Bde on their left, along railway through H.22 central.

7th S.R. lines allotted as follows.

- "A" Coy. G.30.d.9.9. — hedge at H.25.b. central.
- "B" " Thence — Eastern edge of coppice at H.26.a.4.8.
- "C" " Thence — bridge exclusive.
- "D" " In reserve about H.19.d central.
- Bn HQ. On main road immediately N of "D" coy.

TASK 1

You are sent back as company representative of "C" coy to select position for your company.

How would you distribute the company — 4 platoons and Coy. H.Q.?

TASK 2

Time is 2000. You have half an hours daylight left after selecting your company line. At the road corner is a runner post of 4 men, and with them 4 men of an H.L.I Bn, who state that they have lost their Bn.

How would you best utilise your time?

You have been ordered to meet the company at the bridge any time after 2130.

The Railway Bridge is now demolished.

TASK 3

As platoon commander of the forward platoon, describe in detail exactly how the platoon would be disposed, and what cover if any you would order.

The strength of your platoon is as follows:-

L.G. Section	1 L/cpl	4 men
Bombers		2 men
Rifle grenadiers	1 cpl	5 men
Infantry		7 men
H.Q. of platoon	1 signaller & your batman	

TASK 4

Same as task 3, Taking left platoon.

Strength L.G.	1 NCO	2 men
Bombers		8 men
Rifle grenadiers	1 N.CO	4 men
Infantry	2 NCOs	6 men
H.P.	1 signaller	2 runners

It is now Z a.m.

TASK 5

You are platoon commander of the left platoon. General action is taking place along the whole front since 0700. No living Boche is in sight over the crest beyond LA GRANDE LYS, though several abortive attacks have been made. Your platoon has hardly fired a shot.

The nearest post of the Bn on your left is just beyond the hedge & across the railway, concealed from you by the hedge. There has been heavy rifle fire from this post for about ½ an hour.

At 0815 you suddenly see about 8 Boches come through the hedge halfway between the railway bridge, and the main road.

A. What do you deduce. ?

B. What do you do. ?

C. Write your report to your O.C. coy.

~~It is nearly 7 day~~

~~TASK~~

~~You are a platoon commander of the left platoon.
General action is taking place along the whole front
since 0700. Having both its weight~~

TASK. 6.

How do you move your platoon?
Method and route.

TASK. 7

Give your dispositions in detail.

TASK. 8.

2 Lewis Guns, who report that they have been sent to reinforce your Company arrive at your platoon, stating they missed Coy HQ. on the way down.

What do you do?

No 10 platoon has now prolonged your left across the Road. For the moment there is no movement in front of you.

TASK 9

A single Boche comes down the road to surrender. He states there are 42 others just coming in, and he has been sent forward so that they shall be recognised as surrenderers.

They appear, carrying their rifles above their heads.

How will you receive them.?

TASK 10

For Company Commanders.

½ the reserve coy is sent down to you to use as you consider fit. How do you dispose of them?

Your left platoon has a gap of about 300 yds between it and the 4th R.S.

Operation Order No. 16
by
Lieut. Col. C.E. Romanes D.S.O.
Comdg. 1/7th Bn. The Cameronians (Scottish Rifles)

APPENDIX II

6th May 1918.

1. **Move.** 156th Bde. will move on 8th inst. to NEUVILLE ST. VAAST and will there be in reserve to the Division which is transferred to the 18th Corps and is occupying the MERICOURT Sector.

2. **Transport.** Transport will move by road on 7th May along with train baggage wagons, on which will be carried waterproof sheets, mess stores, Q.M. stores and signallers stores.

Only the minimum amount of baggage may be retained till the 8th inst.

3. **Loading Party.** O.C. B Coy. will detail a loading party of 1 Off. and 30 Other Ranks to report at AIRE Station to Capt. G.S. Smith at 0700 on 8th inst. This party will remain on duty until all baggage of the Bde. group is loaded and will not return to present billets.

4. **Parade.** Battn. will form up in column of route ready to move off at 1515 on 8th inst.

Head of column at cross roads H.20.a.7.2 (81a+36a)

Order of march - Bn.H.Q. B.A.D.C. Coys.

P.T.O.

2.

5. **Billets.** All billets and billeting areas will be left scrupulously clean.

1 Copy to A Coy.
1 " " B "
1 " " C "
1 " " D "
1 " " Q.M.
1 " " T.O.
2 " Diary.

[signature]
Capt. & Adjt.
1/7th Cameronians (Sco. Rifles)

Operation Order No. 17.

Lieut. Col. J.S.E. Romanes D.S.O.
Comdg 1/7th Bn. The Cameronians (Scottish Rifles).

6th May 1918.

1. Move. Coys. will move independently to AIRE Station passing starting point at following times:-
BN.HQ. - 1430.   B Coy. - 1440.   D Coy. - 1500.
A " - 1450.   C " - 1510.
These times must be rigidly adhered to.

Coys. will not halt between starting point and AIRE Station.

This order cancels sub-order No. 4 of Operation Order No. 16.

2. Dress. One blanket and greatcoat will be carried in pack.

One blanket per man will be rolled in bundles of 10 and dumped at Q.M. Store at an hour to be notified later.

O.C. Coys. are personally responsible that not more than one blanket per man are handed in to Q.M. Store for carriage.

3. Water. Water bottles will be filled before leaving RIMCQ.

1 Copy to A Coy.   1 Copy to Q.M.
1 "   B   1 " T.O.
1 "   C   2 Diary.
1 "   D

Hector Roche
Capt. & Adjt.
1/7th Cameronians
(Sco. Rifles)

APPENDIX "III".

Training Programme.
1/7th Cameronians (Sco. Rifles).

1918.

Hours	Thurs. 9th May	Frid. 10th May	Sat. 11th May	Mon. 13th May	Tues. 14th May	Wed. 15th May
0400	Close Order Drill	Close Order Drill	Close Order Drill	Close Order Drill	Close Order Drill	Close Order Drill
0800	Normal Formation for Attack.	Bayonet Fighting	Normal Formation for Attack.	Bayonet Fighting	Normal Formation for Attack.	Bayonet Fighting
1000	Bayonet Fighting Musketry	Bayonet Fighting Musketry	Bayonet Fighting Musketry	Bayonet Fighting Musketry	Bayonet Fighting Musketry	Bayonet Fighting Musketry
1230	Close Order Drill	Close Order Drill	Close Order Drill	Close Order Drill	Close Order Drill	Close Order Drill
1400	L. Gun Training	L. Gun Training	L. Gun Training	L. Gun Training	L. Gun Training	L. Gun Training
1530	Bayonet Fighting Musketry	Bayonet Fighting Musketry	Bayonet Fighting Musketry	Bayonet Fighting Musketry	Bayonet Fighting Musketry	Bayonet Fighting Musketry

Note. Box Respirators to be worn frequently and men practised in all duties while wearing them.
Simple Tactical Schemes for N.C.Os.

Capt. & adjt.
1/7th Cameronians
(Scot. Rif.)

Operation Order No. 18
by
Lieut. Col. J. W. P. Romanes D.S.O.
Comdg. 1/7th Bn. The Cameronians (Scottish Rifles).

Ref. Map Fort Hill 13th Edition 20,000.   15th May 1918.

1. **Relief.**   Battn. will probably take over the sector of the line occupied by the 1/5th K.O.S.B. on the night of 15/16th inst. This sector extends from B.10.b.5.7. on the South to T.28.d.5.6. on the North.

    The front line is held by 2 Companies, the Right Coy. holding from Southern point of Battn. sector to road in B.4.b.4.2. inclusive, and the left Coy. holding the remainder of the line.

    These Coys. have 3 platoons in the line and 1 platoon in close support.

    The remaining 2 Companies of the Battn. will be in support, one in the neighbourhood of WOILLERVAL and the other at B.4.a.3.5. approximately.

    Battn. H.Q. are at B.9.a.8.6.
    Battn. Aid Post is at B.9.c.0.3.

2. **Disposition.**   Coys. will be disposed as follows:-

    In the Line   -   B Coy. on the Left.
                     D   "   "   Right.
    In Support   -   A   "   "   Left.
                     C   "   "   Right.

    O.C. Coys. will reconnoitre the line tomorrow.

3. **Rations.**   The right supporting Company will provide the ration carrying party for the Battn. Full orders on this point will be given later.

4. **Dress.**   Men will proceed to the line in Fighting Order (as already laid down) but will wear greatcoats. No blankets will be taken.

    Officers may take such kit as they can carry.

1 copy to A Coy.
1   "   B "
1   "   C "
1   "   D "
1   "   H.Q.
1   "   M.O.
2   "   Diary.

Capt. & Adjt.
1/7th Cameronians (Sco. Rifles)

Trench Standing Orders.

APPENDIX V

1. The garrison of the firing line will wear equipment at all times. The garrison of the support line will wear equipment at night only, excepting men on duty who will invariably wear equipment.

2. No man will leave his platoon or section area to proceed to another part of the line without permission from commander concerned.

3. An officer of each Coy. forming garrison of firing line will invariably be on duty. He must, during his tour of duty, remain constantly in the firing line and will visit all sentries in his sector very frequently. He may leave firing line only to visit sentries in the support line.

4. All sentries must be conversant with their duties. The officer on duty will be responsible for ensuring this.

5. All ranks must keep themselves smart, clean and tidy and be shaved daily by 1000.

6. Trenches must be kept scrupulously clean. No rubbish will be thrown over the parapet or parados.

7. All ranks must be carefully instructed in the use and meaning of gas alarms.

8. Strict attention must be paid to saluting. There should be no slacking off in this respect because the Battn. is in the line.

9. All ranks concerned will be warned about rules governing the use of the telephone.

10. O.C. Coys. will ensure that a proper runner system is established and maintained.

11. It must be impressed on all ranks that the greatest vigilance is essential.

Capt. & Adjt.
Cameronians
(Sco. Rifles)

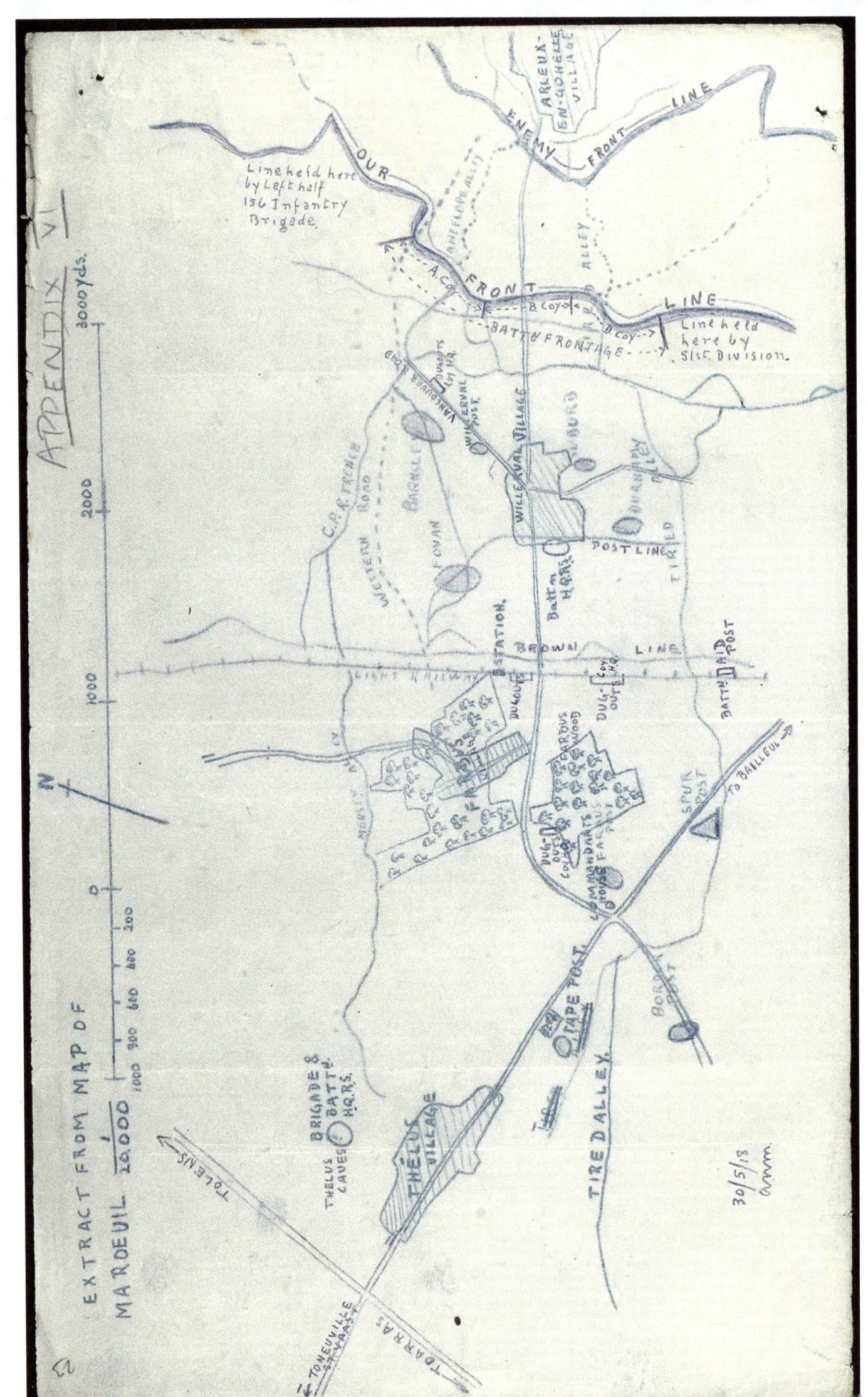

Army Form C. 2118.

WAR DIARY
INTELLIGENCE SUMMARY.
(Erase heading not required.)

CONFIDENTIAL

WAR DIARY

FOR

JUNE 1918.

1/4th Battn The Cameronians (Scottish Rifles)

Volume XXXVII

Vol 3

WAR DIARY
or
INTELLIGENCE SUMMARY.
(Erase heading not required.)

Army Form C. 2118.

A(1)

	Officers	Other Ranks	Remarks
Strength in the Field at 31st May	32	682	
" " 30th June	31	666	

Alterations in Strength during Month.

	Off.	O.R.'s	
Increase			
Reinforcements	-	81	Officers: Major Coughton Fisher to O.C. Train Comms. Col. Jeff. Romans from Leave
From Hospital	-	90	2/Lt. W. Audrep " "
Detachments	14	49	Capt. J. Phillips " " — Course
Other Causes	—	—	2/Lt. G. Brooks " "
	14	214	Capt. R.C. Arthur " "
			2/Lt. W.J. Atkinson " "
			" R.S. Neil " " Traffic Control
			Capt. J. Bain " "
			2/Lt. J. Cullen " " Leave
			2/Lt. D. Renton " "
Decrease			
Killed	—	—	Decrease
Wounded	—	3	2/Lt. G.E.H. Hamman to Red Hospital
Gassed	—	5	" J. Chapter to Lourve
Hospital (sick)	1	106	" F. Dhren do
Courses	6	34	Capt. McNelson do
Leave	5	69	Lt. R. Barr do
Other Causes	3	15	Guests Officer do (England)
	15	230	2/Lt. R. Fenton 69 training centre Frankton
			" W.R. Burns to H.Q training centre Frankton
			2/Lt. Ec. Neild — Traffic Control
			" E.D. Cobbs — Sub Depot School
			Lt Col. J. Thomas A.D.O.S. — Leave
			" J. Laurie " "
			" L. Graydon " "
			Capt. J.R. Spence " "

Ref: attack facing from MAROEUIL 1:20000 (Appendix I)
France Sheet 51b 1:40000
1:40000

Army Form C. 2118.

WAR DIARY
or
INTELLIGENCE SUMMARY.
(Erase heading not required.)

A.(2)

June 1918

Place	Date	Hour	Summary of Events and Information	Remarks and references to Appendices
RESERVE TRENCHES (THELUS)	1		Continued fine weather. Artillery and aerial activity on both sides normal during the night. During the day the enemy artillery shewed more activity from the right. Post and coy H.Q. of right Coy of the Bath was carried out without incident.	Appendix I
	2		Light sentry relief line carried out and then artillery was abnormally quiet. After no transfer Battns of our relief coy were taken in lorries to OTTAWA CAMP, MONT ST ELOY. relief companies were taken in lorries to OTTAWA CAMP, MONT ST ELOY. Lieut.Col. J.G.P. ROMANES, D.S.O. Took over command of 15th Infantry Bde. the Brigadier being on leave to U.K. MAJOR R. BLAIR assumed command during the time Lt. Bath. has been in his hands the Batt. nuclei had remained in camp at VILLERS AU BOIS under Major R. BLAIR. Training was carried out daily in the vicinity of the camp was shelled occasionally with high velocity long range guns. The transport and QM's party remained at BERTONVAL FARM. The Bath. details and transport returned to OTTAWA CAMP.	
MONT ST ELOY	3		The Brigade is in Divisional Reserve and the Battalion is on two hours notice to move. No event in training and refitting. Training programme the day was wholly to companies for the morning's work. "A and B Coys on Refitting (comprehensive of kitting) and clothing and disinfection of blankets and contact patrols commenced. Musketry practice between Regimental squadron and corps tankies and others on trenches to the morning. At 16.00, an officer from Tank Corps lectured to all officers.	Appendix II, Appendix III

Army Form C. 2118.

Map Reference, FRANCE - Sheets 51b & 36b + Material

WAR DIARY or INTELLIGENCE SUMMARY.
(Erase heading not required.)

G.(3)

Place	Date JUNE	Hour	Summary of Events and Information	Remarks and references to Appendices
MONT ST ELOY.	5th		Training carried out according to programme. Inoculation. Battalion on Bde Duty. Bathing carried out at BERTHONVAL.	A.825.f.
	6th		Scheme for co operation with tanks, carried out in the morning at BERTHONVAL, which proved very interesting. Lt Col G.M. Romans D.S.O. resumed command of the Battalion.	A.825.f.
	7th		Orders received for the Battalion to relieve 5.K.O.S.B. in the left sector, right subsector on the 11th June. Training. Inoculation.	A.825.f.
	8th		Training in the forenoon. The line to be taken over on 11th reconnoitred by Battalion and Company representatives.	A.825.f.
	9th	0030	Battalion inspection by the Commanding Officer.	A.825.f.
		1100	Church Parade in Y.M.C.A Hut, OTTOWA CAMP. (Rev. [Spencer]. C.F.)	
	10th		Major R.Blair assumed command of the Battalion, owing to the absence of Lt Col. G. Romans. D.S.O. on leave U.K. The Advance Party (Nucleus) proceeded up the line at 2.30 p.m. to LA FOLIE FARM.	Annex 1
	11th	0845	Move commenced by motor lorry to DALY CAMP. Relief of 5th Bn. KOSB in right subsector left sector complete by 3.30 p.m. The remainder of today and night was quiet. For disposition see Appendix IV. During the transport and Q.M. party moved to DALY CAMP (A.12.a.6.3) and the Battalion nucleus under Capt Bow to VILLERS CAMP. VILLERS AU BOIS. (X.24.d.8.b.)	APPENDIX IV. APPENDIX IV.a & IV.b. Annex 1

Army Form C. 2118.

FRANCE – Sheets 51a.a.36.b + Marcoint
Ref. attached facing April 1 **WAR DIARY**
of
Instructions regarding War Diaries and Intelligence
Summaries are contained in F. S. Regs., Part II.
and the Staff Manual respectively. Title pages
will be prepared in manuscript.

INTELLIGENCE SUMMARY

June 1918.   A (4)

(Erase heading not required.)

Place	Date	Hour	Summary of Events and Information	Remarks and references to Appendices
Front Line Trenches	12		Quiet day and little enemy movement seen except in MERICOURT and ACHEVILLE. Our planes active and artillery carried out several shoots. Patrols from "A" and "C" Coys. – afternoon	Patrol Reports. See APPENDIX V.
	13		Poor observation. A few 77 mm. shells in "A" Coy sector during the afternoon; no damage done. One enemy aeroplane flying low was driven off by Lewis Gun fire. 2/Lt. N. S. YHOMSON to Hospital. 1st SOS. on "C" Coy sector responded to within one minute of message being reported through to artillery. Patrols from "B" and "C" Coys – afternoon.	
	14	0130	"B" Coy Support line why 3. Target (GERRARD). One other rank wounded. More hostile artillery activity but no damage done. From 0300 to 0330 the area round Batt. H.Q. was bombarded with light H.E. Seven shells fell in the Quarry (T.16.c)	
	15		Usual enemy movement observed in MERICOURT and ACHEVILLE Patrol reports appended.	
	16		A quiet day in Battalion sector with little hostile artillery activity. Our artillery very active during the night on targets in back areas. Patrols appended. Low flying enemy aircraft over our lines in the morning engaged by Lewis Gun fire.	

Army Form C. 2118.

Map Ref. FRANCE Sheets 51c & 36b. Mericourt
and attached tracing appendix I

WAR DIARY
or
INTELLIGENCE SUMMARY.   A (5)
(Erase heading not required.)

Instructions regarding War Diaries and Intelligence
Summaries are contained in F. S. Regs., Part II.
and the Staff Manual respectively. Title pages
will be prepared in manuscript.

Place	Date	Hour	Summary of Events and Information	Remarks and references to Appendices
Front Line trenches			Our heavies active on MERICOURT, ACHEVILLE, and enemy front line system. Enemy exceptionally quiet. A few H.E. in T.16.c. in the afternoon. Considerable movement in ACHEVILLE during the afternoon, dealt with by our artillery. Two other ranks (U.S.A. Army. 80th Division) attached for instruction. Patrols afforded.	For latest Patrol Reports see APPENDIX I.
	17		Enemy low flying aircraft over Battalion sector in the morning engaged by Lewis Gun fire. Vicinity of Battn. H.E. shelled in the afternoon with about 30 4.1's. Little hostile artillery activity. Our guns active at night. Patrols afforded.	
	18		One hostile aircraft over Battalion sector in early morning engaged by Lewis Gun fire. Hostile artillery more active. About fifty 5.9's in vicinity of NEW BRUNSWICK Trench. No damage done. Patrols afforded. Quiet morning. Artillery on both sides more active in the afternoon. By our heavies.	
	19.	10 pm. 11.15 pm	Battn. H.Q. again shelled. On fire covering the hostile battery was engaged. GERRARD Trench shelled – 1 other rank killed. Vest S.O.S. – answered in three minutes.	6

Army Form C. 2118.

WAR DIARY
INTELLIGENCE SUMMARY
(Erase heading not required.)

FRANCE Sheets 51c & 36b. Maroeuil   A (6)

Place	Date	Hour	Summary of Events and Information	Remarks and references to Appendices
Roeust trenches	20		Batt. relieved by 14th Batt. 4/R. Royal Scots and moved into billets in VIMY area. Relief completed by 3.30 p.m. Dispositions as in attached facing. The nine days spent in the line were very quiet and the Batt. suffered only two casualties. Hostile artillery was on the whole inactive in the Batt. sector. Patrols were out nightly but on no occasion were enemy patrols encountered. Enemy troops opposite belonged to 12th (Res) Division.	APPENDIX VI + VIa for patrol reports see APPENDIX V
	21		Companies wiring and digging in their respective areas. GRAND TRUNK trench ("A" Coy area) shelled in the afternoon and one rank killed.	
	22		Wiring and digging continued in Battalion Sector.	
	23		Work continued. Hostile artillery more active during the day. Night about 15 rounds 4.2" in Battn. H.QRS. area. About midnight. No damage was done.	
	24		Work carried out during the day. Aeroplanes very active. Artillery carried out several shoots. Very active at night, during the early part of which hostile back areas were heavily shelled with gas. Thereinwas no retaliation on the Battalion sector.	
	25		About 2 p.m. about D'RENTON sent one platoon went to 1st Army School at MATRINGHEM. A very quiet morning - work as usual. Enemy shelled our batteries in VIMY in the afternoon without success.	
	26		Enemy carried out shorts against our batteries near the LENS - ARRAS ROAD. LA CHAUDIERE shelled in the morning. Aeroplanes active in the evening. Our guns carried out harassing fire throughout the night.	

Mont Noir France Sheets 51a & 36b
& Maroeuil

WAR DIARY
of
INTELLIGENCE SUMMARY.
(Erase heading not required.)

Army Form C.2118.

A (7)

Place	Date 1918	Hour	Summary of Events and Information	Remarks and references to Appendices
RESERVE TRENCHES	June 27		A quiet day with little aerial or artillery activity on either side. During the day our "B" + "C" Companies were relieved by the 1/4th Royal Scots in view that these companies could relieve the 1/9th Scottish Rifles who were unable to the 1/9th Royal Scots + who were leaving the Brigade. This relief of the 2nd Scottish Rifles was carried out late (See Appendix VI) first A.E. Raid temporarily attached Bde H.Q. (A/I.O)	Annexure APPENDIX VI
	28		The day passed quietly. Nothing to report.	Annexure
	29		During the day the battalion was relieved by the 1/5th H.L.I. The relief passed off without incident beyond the fact that the enemy shot down a few shrapnel shells. There were no casualties. The Battalion proceeded to OTTAWA CAMP, MONT ST ELOI as formerly. Lt-Col. J.G. Romanus D.S.O. took over command. Battalion Runners, Batn H.Q. Signallers from the trenches, the transport remained at DALY CAMP. Runners and the nucleus at VILLERS AU BOIS + today returned to OTTAWA CAMP. Depôt 17 46 and 29 other ranks reported to the nucleus while the battalion was in the line.	APPENDIX VII Annexure
MONT ST ELOI	30		This day was spent bathing & cleaning up. An the evening afternoon the 4th Royal Berks (the Yet C anteroom was held preparatory to an inspection by the Duke of Connaught tomorrow. 2Lt D Paxton + his platoon returned from 1st Army School MATRINGHEM.	Annexure

K.M. Fox, Captain
Commanding 1/4th Bn Cameronians
(S.R.)

8

APPENDIX I

Extract from
MARDEUIL
1/20000

Operation order APPENDIX II
by
Lt. Col. J. M. Romanes D.S.O. Commanding
1/7th Cameronians (Scottish Rifles), 1st June 1918

Relief. Battalion will be relieved by 7th H.L.I. on 3rd June. Coys will be relieved as under:-
D Coy 7th H.L.I. relieves B Coy 1/7th S.R.
B " " " " D " "
C " " " " C " "
A " " " " A " "

Note:- A Coy of 7th H.L.I. will move into BROWN LINE and not FARBUS WOOD. A Coy of 1/7th S.R. will move all L.G's and equipment tomorrow night to dug out at present occupied by 1st Canadian Tunnelling Coy and will leave them there with adequate guard. Nos. 1 & 2 of guns will accompany the guns.

Lewis Gun Magazines. Lewis Gun Magazines and tin boxes will be exchanged. Leather cases (empty) will be taken away. O.C. A Coy will detail an Officer to effect exchange in BROWN LINE and to march guard back to Camp.

New Camp. On completion of relief Coys will move independently to OTTAWA CAMP and will occupy same huts as formerly. Completion of relief will be notified by code word RUPERT. This will be sent with the utmost expedition. O.C. C Coy will notify 1/4th Royal Scots

- 2 -

Movement. On moving down platoons will move at 400 yards distance. In event of Coys meeting on the road, order of precedence will be D. B. A. C. O.C. A Coy will take greatest care in leaving FARBUS WOOD to avoid congestion.

Receipts. Receipts for stores handed over will reach Battalion H.Q. by 1000 on 3rd inst. made out in duplicate on usual pro forma.

Discipline. Strict March discipline must be maintained on road down.

Guides. O.C. B Coy will detail 8 men, O.C. C Coy 4 men, O.C. D Coy 4 men, to report to Intelligence Officer at Battn. H.Q. at 0800 on 3rd inst. to act as guides.

Chain. Bde. Chain of Guides will be arranged by Intelligence Officer.

Routes. C, D & A Coy will move back via TIRED ALLEY. B Coy via MERSEY ALLEY.

Capt & Adjt
1/4th Cameronians
(Sco. Rifles)

APPENDIX III

Programme of Training

Time	1st Day	2nd Day	3rd Day	4th Day	5th Day	6th Day
0700						
0800	Physical Training & Close Order Drill					
0815	Breakfast					
0900	Company Orderly Room					
0945	Battⁿ — Do —					
1000	Platoon at disposal of Platoon Commander					
1230	Musketry – Bayonet Fighting – Simple Tactical Exercises					
1245	Lunch					
1400	Lewis Gun Training					
1530	Tactical Schemes for Officers & N.C.O.s					
1700	Dinner					

23/3/18

Hector Maclean
Capt & Adjt
for O.C. 1/7 Cameronians
(Scot. Rifles)

Operation Orders No. 20 APPENDIX IV.a

Lieut Col. J.G.P. Romanes, D.S.O.
Commanding 7th The Cameronians (Scottish Rifles)

7th June 1918

1. Battalion will relieve 1/5th KOSB in the left sector, right sub-section, on the 11th inst.

2. This sub-section is held by three companies in front line and immediate support, and one company in reserve.

3. Companies will take over as under:—

   "C" Coy. 7th S.R. from "C" Coy. 5th KOSB (left of the line)
   "B" Coy. 7th S.R. from "B" Coy. 5th KOSB (centre of the line)
   "A" Coy. 7th S.R. from "D" Coy. 5th KOSB (right of line)
   "D" Coy. 7th S.R. from "A" Coy. 5th KOSB (in reserve)

4. Company Officers will reconnoitre the parts of the line they will be taking over as soon as possible.

5. Nominal Rolls should be prepared of men who will be left behind with Details, i.e. surplus to the establishment of 1 N.C.O and 6 men per section.

6. Captain BOW will be in charge of Details.

Capt. & Adjt.
Cameronians
(Scottish Rifles)

14. All Companies should frequently practise the manning of trenches from deep dug-outs.

15. Every effort should be made to salve as much as possible. Salved articles should be taken to Battalion H.Q.

16. The importance of rendering returns so as to reach Brigade H.Q. by hour indicated is to be brought to notice. The undermentioned are required daily:

   Situation ....
   Intelligence .... 8 a.m. and 6 p.m.
   Work and Progress .... 10 a.m.
   Casualty .... 12 noon
   Strength .... 12 noon
   Inspection of S.A.A.etc. 12 noon

17. All points laid down in 52nd Divisional Trench Standing Orders will be carefully observed.

                                    [signature]
                                    Major
                                    Comdg. The Cameronians
                                    (Scottish Rifles)

APPENDIX V.

1st The Cameronians.

Patrols – 11-6-18 to 20-6-18.
Reference MAROEUIL. 1/20,000.

12-6-18.

1). 1 officer, 2/Lt Cullen, with 2 sections "C" coy, left our lines at T.10.c.6.0. at 10.30 p.m. and proceeded to T.11.a.4.3.
Hostile post at T.11.a.5.3. was reconnoitred, but found unoccupied, nor were there signs of recent occupation. Patrol returned at 12.30 a.m.

2). 1 officer 2/Lt Hood, with 2 sections "A" coy, left our lines about T.17.c.10.4 at 1 a.m. The wire in front of TOTNES TRENCH was found to be very thick, and no gaps could be found. Patrol was unable to proceed, and returned about 3.a.m.

13-6-18.

1). 1 officer, 2/Lt McQueen, and 2 sections "C" coy, left our lines about T.16.c.4.1 at 11.30 p.m., and proceeded to T.11.a.4.4.
Post at T.11.b.5.1 was reconnoitred but was found to be unoccupied. Patrol returned at 1.a.m.

2). 1 officer, 2/Lt Sniges, and 2 sections "B" coy, left our lines about T.16.a.2.8, at 1 a.m., and proceeded to T.18.a.0.4. No enemy were seen. It was found impossible to examine the wire, owing to the number of flares put up by the enemy. Hostile machine guns were active.
Patrol returned at 3.a.m.

14-6-18.

1). 1 officer 2/Lt Strathearn, and 2 sections "C" coy, left our lines about T.10.c.6.0 at 11 p.m. and proceeded to post at T.11.a.5.1, which was unoccupied. Patrol proceeded to enemy wire at about T.11.a.8.4. The wire at this point was found to be very strong, at least two belts being observed. A machine gun was active immediately beyond the wire.
Attempts were made without success to find a gap, and patrol returned to our lines about 2.a.m.

15-6-18.

1). 1 Officer 2/Lt Renton, and 2 sections "C" coy left our lines at T.10.b.2.4 at 1 a.m., and proceeded along N side of the MERICOURT ROAD to about T.11.a.4.3. Post at T.11.a.5.1 was not occupied, and patrol proceeded to wire at about T.11.a.8.3. No gaps were found in this wire which was strong. A machine gun from the direction of MERICOURT, fired bursts along the wire at this point. Patrol saw no enemy, and returned at 3.a.m.

2). 1 Officer 2/Lt Gillies, and 2 sections "A" coy, left our lines at 12.15 a.m., and proceeded through gap cut in our wire, to enemy wire about T.18.a.2.10. A trip wire was found immediately in front of the main belt. The wire was examined to about T.18.a.2.4, without finding any gaps. Machine gun fire from OBREST TRENCH, went very high. No enemy seen. Patrol returned at 3 a.m.

16-6-18.

D. 1 Officer, 2/Lt Hood, and 2 sections "A" coy left our lines at about T.17.a.7.2 at 12 p.m., and proceeded along old railway track to about T.18.a.2.0, when movement was heard ahead, which sounded like wooden stakes being driven in. Patrol halted, and O.C. and 2 other ranks proceeded along N side of MOOSEJAW RD. Enemy party about 20 observed working inside the enemy wire. This party moved a short distance E, and recommenced work. No gaps were seen in wire. Patrol returned at 2.45 a.m.

17-6-18.

2 Officers 2/Lt Singer and 2/Lt W.T. Anderson, with 2 sections 1 Lewis gun, and 2 Bn Scouts left our lines at T.17.a.8.3, and proceeded to T.12.c.0.0, in order to scupper and secure identification from any working party repairing the wire damaged by our artillery during the day.

The enemy appeared to be suspicious, as the wire was continuously raked with machine gun fire, and large numbers of flares were put up.

No movement of any kind was observed. Three blasts of a whistle was heard.

Patrol returned at 2.a.m.

3.

18-6-18

2 Officers Lt H J Forbes, and Lt W.T. Anderson, with 2 sections "B" coy, one Lewis gun, and 2 Bn Scouts, proceeded to T.18.a.4.5; at 11 p.m., in order to secure identification from any working party repairing wire damaged by our artillery during the day.

Scouts were pushed forward. 2 men were observed coming through a gate in the second belt. They crawled through the front belt and lay down in front. One man remained behind the wire. The scout could not move on account of the men behind the wire and consequently could not warn the patrol that the two others were outside.

These men lay for an hour, then withdrew. No further movement was observed, and patrol withdrew at 2.30 a.m.

20-6-18.

(1 Lewis gun)
1 Officer, Lieut. A. W Bird, and 2 sections "D" coy with 8 Bn Scouts and 1 American O.R. attached left 12th AVENUE at 10.45 p.m, for the purpose of scuppering and securing identification from any working party repairing the wire damaged by our artillery.

Patrol proceeded along the old railway lines for about 400 yds then branched off to the left and took up a position about 40 yds in front of the wire at about T.12.c.0.1.

The front belt of wire did not appear to have been damaged by the bombardment and no movement of any description was seen. Two machine guns fired short bursts from about T.18.a.5.6 and T.12.c.2.3 respectively, both in a N.W direction.

Patrol returned to our lines at 2.30 a.m.

APPENDIX VI.

SUPPORT BATTALION.
VIMY – LA CHAUDIERE AREA.
LEFT & RIGHT – C.B.D. and B Coys.

Battalion H.Q.
Company area
HQ Platoon

Scale 1/10,000

Army Form C. 2118.

WAR DIARY
INTELLIGENCE SUMMARY.
(Erase heading not required.)

Vol 4

1/7th CAMERONIANS (S.R.)

WAR DIARY
for
JULY 1915

Confidential

Place	Date	Hour	Summary of Events and Information	Remarks and references to Appendices

Reference Maps:
M4 ROEUIL 1/10,000
FRANCE SHEET 44B $\frac{20,000}{40,000}$ "28
– do – 44A

Army Form C. 2118.

WAR DIARY
or
INTELLIGENCE SUMMARY.
(Erase heading not required.)

July 1918.

Instructions regarding War Diaries and Intelligence Summaries are contained in F. S. Regs., Part II. and the Staff Manual respectively. Title pages will be prepared in manuscript.

Place	Date	Hour	Summary of Events and Information	Remarks and references to Appendices
Mont St. Eloy.	1.		Lt. Col. Romanes D.S.O. took over command of Battalion. The Brigade was inspected by H.R.H. The Duke of Connaught in the morning.	
	2.		Capt. Mather took over command of the Battalion from Major Blair who proceeded to Senior Officers School Aldershot.	
	3.		Training was carried out as per programme.	Appendix 1.
	4.		– do –	
	5.		– do –	
	6.		– do –	
	7.		Church service was held in Y.M.C.A. hut in Ottawa Camp in the morning. Advance party proceeded to front line (Willerval Sector)	Appendix 2.
Willerval Sector.	8.		Lt. Col. Romanes D.S.O. re-assumed command of the Battalion. Battalion took over the Willerval Sector from the 1/5th Royal Scots Fus. Transport proceeded to Latta Camp (A.7.a.1.4.) & the Nucleus Coy to Villers Camp, Villers au Bois.	Appendix 2 & 3.
	9.		Quiet day, at night 2nd/Bn. Gillies patrolled to B5.a.35.35. & B5.a.0.2. no enemy were seen.	
	10.		An enemy AEROPLANE was brought down at T.26.d.1.0. by one of our AEROPLANES.	
	11.		Quiet day & fine weather continued. 2nd Lt. Watson & 2 Rifle Sections patrolled to B.4.B.6.3. no enemy were seen.	
	12.		Quiet day & fine weather continued.	
	13.		2nd Lt. Gordon & 2 Rifle Sections patrolled No Mans Land, enemy encountered when our patrol was leaving trench & fire was opened by our patrol on them, no casualties on either side.	
	14.		Weather broke down.	
	15.		The Battalion was relieved in the Arleux-Willerval Sector by the 47th Canadian Regiment & 50th Canadian Regiment. Our tour of the trenches this time was very quiet with little enemy activity of any kind. The Battalion proceeded to take over new location in Brown Line in vicinity of Vimy. No further particulars can be given the town is unnamed.	Appendix 4 & 5.

Army Form C. 2118.

WAR DIARY or INTELLIGENCE SUMMARY.

MAROEUIL 1:20,000. FRANCE SHEET 44B. 1:20,000 FRANCE SHEET 44A. 1:10,000

(Erase heading not required)

July 1918.

Place	Date	Hour	Summary of Events and Information	Remarks and references to Appendices
BROWN LINE. VIMY.	16.		Good weather continues, Enemy shelled batteries in VIMY.	nil
	17.		Very quiet day.	nil
	18.		- do - Still good weather.	nil
	19.			nil
	20.		Enemy artillery fairly active on VIMY, otherwise quiet day.	nil
	21.		Fine weather.	Appendix.
	22.		The Battalion was relieved by the 2nd. Bn. WEST YORKS & on relief proceeded to MONT ST. ELOY (OTTOWA CAMP) [F.I.D.9.2.]	6 nil
MONT ST. ELOY.	22.		The Battalion was inspected by the Corps Commander, LT. GENERAL SIR A. HUNTER WESTON, & immediately after marched to BOIS d'OLHAIN. The Battalion is now on G.H.Q. RESERVE on 4 hours notice to move. Q.2.d.2.2.	Appendix.
BOIS d'OLHAIN	23.		The day was spent in bathing rebrewing up.	7 + 7ª Annex
	24.		Training carried out per programme.	nil
	25.		Weather has now broken down, training carried on.	nil
	26.		- do -	nil
	27.		- do -	Appendix
	28.		- do -	8 nil
	29.		Weather improved, The Battalion spent all day at the Rifle Range.	nil
ECOIVES.	30		Church Parade was held in the morning. At noon orders were received for the Battalion to proceed to ECOIVES. Advance party proceeded to Reinforcement camp there. Battalion marched to reinforcement camps.	Appendix. 9.
	31.		↳ BRANT CAMPS, ECOIVES. (F.14.A.3.3.) Battalion proceeded to the front line to take over from 54TH. CANADIAN BATTALION in BRIGADE. B.28 and B.29 and in H.3,4 a 5.	nil

D. D. & L., London, E.C.
(A5 04) Wt W177/M2031 750,000 5/17 Sch. 52 Forms/C2116/14

Army Form C. 2118.

WAR DIARY
or
INTELLIGENCE SUMMARY.
(Erase heading not required.)

Instructions regarding War Diaries and Intelligence Summaries are contained in F. S. Regs., Part II. and the Staff Manual respectively. Title pages will be prepared in manuscript.

Place	Date	Hour	Summary of Events and Information	Remarks and references to Appendices

			Strength in the Field. 30th June 1918. O. O.R.
			 " " " " 31st July 1918. 31. 666.
			                                         30. 852.
			                        1 Decrease. 186.(Increase)
			
			 Increase. O. O.R. Officers. Increases.
			 Reinforcements. 1. 136. 2/Lt. L. J. Watson joined from Course.
			 From Hospital. — 46. " H. Chrystal " do.
			 Detachments 235. " H. J. Slocum " do.
			 Other Causes. 14. 235. Capt. G. A. Nelson " do.
			                  15. 417. 2/Lt. St. Kenton " do.
			                              " W. M. Boyd " Leave.
			 Decrease. O. O.R. Capts. A. G. Mullan " "
			 To Hospital. 1. 80. 2/Lt. L. McWilliam " "
			 Killed. — — Lt. J. Smith " "
			 Wounded. — 4. 2/Lt. Col. J.A.P. Romanes " attachment.
			 Courses. 2. 19. Lt. Col. Bird " "
			 Leave. 7. 103. " H. J. Hosken " Leave.
			 Other Causes. 6. 25. Lt. J. G. Bird " "
			                  16. 231. Capt. J. R. Spence.
			                                    Officers Decrease. Capt. A.B. Nicol to 30 Div.
			                            2/Lt. G. Gillies to Hosp. Lt.Col. J.A.P. Romanes. "Bde Employ.
			                           Major R. Klein " Course. Lt. H. Bird " do.
			                           Lt. H. Gunlop " Leave.
			                           Capt. S. McWilliam " "
			                           Capts. W. Mather " "
			                           " W. Lt. Wilson " "
			                           Lt. H. J. Bird " "
			                           " H. J. Hosken " Bde Employ.
			                           " C. B. Gray " "
			                           " R. Barr " R.A.F.
			                           2/Lt. J.O.B. Singer " M.G. Training Centre.
			                           " St. Renton.	

Appendix 11

Training Programme

	Wednesday 3rd	Thursday 4th	Friday 5th	Saturday 6th
8.30 – 9.30	Bayonet fighting Platoon & Company Drill	Route March (7 miles)	Bayonet fighting Platoon & Company Drill	Bayonet fighting Platoon & Company Drill
9.30 – 10.30	Lewis Gun Musketry Physical Training		Lewis Gun Musketry Physical Training	Lewis Gun Musketry Physical Training
10.30 – 11.30	Extended Order Drill Short Tactical Scheme		Extended Order Drill Short Tactical Scheme	Extended Order Drill Short Tactical Scheme

Training of Battalion Scouts Signallers to be carried out daily. Tactical scheme for all available Officers under Commanding Officer on Tuesday morning – scheme to be repeated by P.C. boys with N.C.Os on Friday morning.

Operation Orders
by
Capt. W. Mather
Comdg. 1/7th Bn. The Cameronians (Sco. Rifles)
6th July 1918.

Ref. Map. MAROEUIL. 1/20,000.

1. Relief. The Battn. will relieve 1/5th R.S.F. in Right Sub-Section of Right Sector of Divisional Sector on 8th July.

Battn. Sub-Section boundaries are as follows:-

On the Left. B.2.d.5.0. to junction of NOME and YUKON trenches (exclusive).

On the Right. TIRED ALLEY (inclusive).

Coys will relieve as under.

    "A" Coy relieves "B" Coy 1/5th R.S.F.
    "B"   Do.   "A"   Do.
    "C"   Do.   "C"   Do.
    "D"   Do.   "D"   Do.

2. Dispositions. Dispositions of Coys. will be as for the 1/5th R.S.F. Coys.

In the Line.

On the Left - "D" Coy. (2 platoons in BLUE LINE and 2 platoons in BLACK LINE).

On the Right - "C" Coy. (2 platoons in BLUE LINE and 2 platoons in BLACK LINE).

Inter Coy boundaries will be B.4.C.7.3.

In WILLERVAL Defences - "A" Coy.
In BROWN LINE - "B" ".

Battn. H.Q. will be at B.8.d.8.9.
Battn. Aid Post at B.9.a.9.6.

3. Advance Parties. Advance Party composed as under will parade at 8.15 a.m. on 7th inst. at Y.M.C.A. This party will proceed by bus to A.11.a.4.7. where they will be met by guides.

    - Battn. Intelligence Officer
    - One Officer per Coy.
    - One N.C.O per platoon
    - Two Battn. Runners.
    - Two Runners per Coy.
    - Two Battn. Signallers.
    - Battn. Scout N.C.O. and four scouts.
    - One L.G. N.C.O. per Coy.
    - Battn. and Coy Gas N.C.Os.

P.T.O.

2.

4. **Move.** Coys. will parade as under on 8th inst.

    "D" Coy. — 9.15 a.m.
    C " — 9.30 a.m.
    BN. H.Q — 9.30 a.m.
    A Coy. — 10 a.m.
    B " — 10.15 a.m. and proceed by bus to A.11.a.4.7.

Embussing Officer — Lieut. J. Austin
Debussing Officer — 2/Lt. A. J. Hood
Dress. Fighting Order with greatcoats.
Guides (1 per platoon and Coy. H.Q) will be at CANADIAN MONUMENT. TIRED ALLEY will be used. Till reaching communication trench platoons will move at 200 yds. distance. On the enemy side of Ridge movement will be by sections.

5. **Completion of Relief.** Relief complete will be wired by code word "BOWLER".

6. **Trench Stores.** All trench stores, maps and defence scheme will be taken over and receipts forwarded to Battn. H.Q in duplicate within 24 hours of relief.

7. **Attack.** In the event of an attack during relief troops will assemble in nearest defences and report to nearest Battn. or Bde. H.Q.

8. **Nucleus.** Nucleus under Capt. R. C. S. Aitken will move to Divn. Reception Camp by 2 p.m. on 8th inst.

9. **Transport.** Transport and Administrative H.Q. will move to IATTA Camp by 2 p.m. on 8th inst.

10. **Billets.** All billets will be left scrupulously clean.

11. **Kits.** All kits, stores and packs will be stacked at Q.M. Stores by 8 a.m. on 8th inst. Stores, etc. for nucleus will be stacked separately by 9 a.m.

12. **Rations.** Rations will be brought up by limber nightly to following points, arriving at approximately 10.15 p.m.

    BN. H.Q. and "B" Coy. — B. 8. b. 7. 9.
    BLACK LINE platoons of C & D Coys. — B. 3. c. 8. 2.
    A Coy. — B. 3. d. 6. 2.
    BLUE LINE platoons of C & D Coys. — B. 4. c. 5. 7.

Coys. will supply their own ration parties.
C.Q.M.Ss. will proceed with rations each night to Coy. H.Q.
Cooking will be done in line at Coy. cook-houses.

13. Water.   Drinking water will be drawn daily from tanks at DURHAM post by Coys. in BLUE and BLACK, water for BROWN LINE will be drawn from LONGWOOD.

Washing water will be drawn from WILLERVAL Wells.

Petrol tins will be taken over.

Daily allowance per man is one gallon.

Coys. will take over water picquets supplied by the Coys. they relieve.

14. Ammunition.   Reserve is at B.9.a.9.6.

15. Discipline.   Trench Standing Orders will be strictly enforced.

Five rounds rapid will be fired by every man each day. In the selection of targets care must be taken to avoid pipe lines, reservoirs, etc.

Gordon Orr
Lieut. & Asst./Adjt.
1/7" Cameronians
(Sco. Rifles)

SECRET.   Copy No. 8

156th INFANTRY BRIGADE ORDER No. 42.

Ref.Map.1:20,000 (MAROEUIL).   5th July 1918.

1. The 156th Infantry Brigade will relieve the 155th Infantry Brigade in the Right Section of the 52nd Division Sector on the 8th & 9th July.

2. Reliefs will take place as follows:-

8th July. 1/7th Sco.Rifles will relieve 1/5th R.S.F. in the Right Sub-Section.
1/4th Royal Scots will relieve 1/4th K.O.S.B. in the Centre Sub-section.
1/7th Royal Scots will relieve 1/4th R.S.F. in the Left Sub-Section.
9th July. 156th T.M.Batt. will relieve 155th T.M.Batt.

3. On 7th July advanced parties consisting of Battalion Intelligence Officers, one Officer per company, one N.C.O. per platoon, two battalion runners, two runners per company, two battalion signallers, battalion scout N.C.O., one Lewis Gun N.C.O. per company, battalion and company Gas N.C.Os., will go into the line. They will be met at 9:15 a.m. by guides from the Battalion Headquarters and companies they are relieving as follows:-
1/7th Sco.Rifles at junction of Plank Road with NEUVILLE ST. VAAST-THELUS ROAD (A.11.a.4.7.)
1/4th Royal Scots and 1/7th Royal Scots at Right Brigade Headquarters (A.3.c.8.5.) at 9:30 a.m.
Three motor lorries will convey advanced parties of 1/7th Royal Scots and 1/7th Sco.Rifles to A.11.a.4.7., leaving FRASER CAMP at 8:45 a.m.

4. On 8th July units will be met by guides from Battalion Headquarters, company Headquarters, and platoons of the units they are relieving as follows:-
4th Royal Scots at A.11.a.4.7. from 9:15 a.m. till 10 a.m.
7th Sco.Rifles at A.11.a.4.7. at 10 a.m.
7th Royal Scots at A.11.a.4.7. at 12:15 p.m.
Lorries will be at OTTAWA CAMP from 9:30 a.m. onwards to convey 1/7th Sco.Rifles, and at FRASER CAMP from 11:45 a.m. for 1/7th Royal Scots.

5. 4th Royal Scots and 156th T.M.Batt. will march from NEUVILLE ST. VAAST.

6. Units will appoint their own embussing and debussing Officers. These Officers will make any necessary alterations in event of enemy shelling, and report by wire or cyclist to Brigade.

7. Left and Centre Battalions will use MERSEY ALLEY Communication Trench. Right Battalion will use TIRED ALLEY.

8. Details of relief and exchange of Lewis Gub Magazines, etc. will be arranged between C.Os. concerned.

9. Till reaching the Communication Trenches, platoons will move at 200 yds. distance. On the enemy side of the Ridge movement will be by sections.

10/

2.

10. Commands of Sub-sections will pass on completion of Battalion relief.

11. Completion of relief will be reported by code word "CRIPPEN".

12. Between passing of Command of Section from G.O.C. 155th Infantry Brigade to O.C. 156th Infantry Brigade and relief of 155th T.M.Batt. by 156th T.M.Batt., 156th T.M.Batt. will be under orders of G.O.C. 155th Infantry Brigade.

12a. In the event of an enemy attack while relief is in progress companies will assemble in the nearest defences and report to the nearest Battalion Commander or Brigade Headquarters.

13. Details of units not proceeding into the line will move to Divisional Reception Camp by 2 p.m. 8th July.

14. Transport will be brigaded at ~~DERNONVAL~~ LATTA by 2 p.m. 8th July.

15. Command of the Section passes on completion of the Infantry relief at which hour Brigade Headquarters will close at WHITE HOUSE, ST.ELOI, and open at Right Section Headquarters.

16. ACKNOWLEDGE.

Issued by Runner at 10 pm   WRKermack Captain,
A/Bde.Major, 156th Inf. Brigade.

Copy No. 1 G.O.C.
        2 4th Royal Scots.
        3 7th Royal Scots.
        4. 7th Sco.Rifles.
        5. 156th T.M.Batt.
        6 Staff Captain.
        7 I.O. & Bde.Sigs.
        8 B.T.O.
        9 52nd Division.
        10 155th Inf.Brigade.
        11 157th Inf.Brigade.
        12 Bde.Supply Officer.
        13 2nd Lowland Field Ambulance.
    14 & 15 War Diary.
        16. File.

SECRET.   No. 1/93/1

         TO all recipients of

              188th INFANTRY BRIGADE ORDER No. 41.
         ==

         Reference Brigade Order No.48, para. 14, for "PERNESVAL"
read "LATNA".

         This will be permanent camp for 188th Bde.Transport. A/Staff
Capt. will allot units areas today at an hour to be notified later.

                                        W R Kermack Captain.
6th July 1918.   A/Bde. Major, 188th Inf.Brigade.

SECRET.   Copy No. 8

BTO

158th Infantry Brigade.

ADMINISTRATIVE ORDERS No. 8.

Ref. 158th Infantry Brigade Order No. 42.

1. **BILLETS AND CAMPS.**
   (i).   All billets and camps will be left absolutely clean before Units march out.
   (ii). Certificates from O.C., Advance Party, of incoming Units that Billets, Camps and horse standings were taken over in a clean and sanitary condition, and a Certificate from the Area Commandant that there are no outstanding claims for damage to Government property, will be sent to Brigade H.Q. by 8 a.m on 8th July.

2. **TRANSPORT AND QUARTERMASTERS STORES.**
   (i).   Units will take over the horse standings and camps allotted to them by the A/Staff Captain at LATTA CAMP and the Camp West of it. They will be vacant by 2 p.m. on 8th July.
   (ii). The B.T.O. will issue any further instructions necessary. He will report completion of move by wire to Bde. H.Q. by code word "PARIS".
   (iii). The B.T.O. will forward to Bde. H.Q. within 48 hours of arrival in Camp a return of stores taken over, made out on Div. Trench Stores Pro Forma.
   (iv). Baggage Wagons of the Divisional Train will report to Units' H.Q. at 6 a.m. on 8th July.

3. **BLANKETS AND OFFICERS' KITS.**
   Blankets and Officers' kits will be conveyed to units' Q.M. Stores LATTA CAMP under their own arrangements.

4. **RATIONS.**
   (i).   Refilling Point, commencing 8th July:-
          LEADLEY SIDING - A.E.G.S.9.
   (ii). Rations will be drawn at 3 p.m. and delivered by the Supply Section of the Train at Units' Q.M. Stores, LATTA CAMP.
   (iii). **DISTRIBUTION.**
          (a). **Right Battalion.**
               3 Companies by limber to R.S.G.S.7.
               1 Coy and Battalion H.Q. by limber to Batln. H.Q.
          (b). **Centre Battalion.**
               3 Coys by limber to Cookhouses, VANCOUVER, T.29.a.4.3.
               1 Coy and Batln. H.Q. by train from ZIVY to MORRISON.
          (c). **Left Battalion.**
               3 Coys by limber to Cookhouses, VANCOUVER, T.29.a.4.3.
          (d). **T.M. Battery.**
               By rail from ZIVY to MORRISON.
          (e). **Brigade H.Q.** ... by Limber.
   (iv). Rations forwarded by light railway will be loaded on trucks at ZIVY by 7.30 p.m. nightly.
   (v).   The B.T.O. will inform Transport Officers the hour at which Transport may proceed over VIMY Ridge.
   (vi). An Officer of each Battalion Administrative H.Q. will proceed with rations each night, and report at their Battalion H.Q.
   (vii). C.Q.M.Ss. will proceed to their Coy H.Q. each night with rations which they will hand over at their Coy Cookhouses.

5. **WATER.**/

2.

5. **WATER.**
   (i). **Right Battalion.**
   　(a). Drinking water is conveyed by Light Railway each
   　　　night to four 200 gall. tanks at DURHAM POST - B.9.b.2.3. -
   　　　filled under Water Supply Officer's arrangements.
   　　　　Battalion H.Q. and 1 Coy draw from LONGWOOD, at
   　　　which there are four 200 gall. tanks, filled each
   　　　night by the Division on the Right.
   　(c). Washing water is drawn from WILLERVAL WELLS.
   (ii). **Centre Battalion.**
   　(a). Drinking water is drawn from MERSEY - B.2.a.8.7. -
   　　　and FARBUS - B.2.d.1.0. - both filled by pipe line.
   　　　Water for 3 forward Coys is filled from MERSEY into
   　　　petrol tins by Battalion Water Picquet by day and
   　　　dumped at B.2.a.7.8. where it is collected by limber
   　　　at night and conveyed to VANCOUVER.
   　(b). If this supply fails, petrol tanks will be filled
   　　　at MORRISON.
   　(c). Washing water may be drawn from FARBUS WOOD WELLS.
   (iii). **Left Battalion.**
   　(a). Drinking water is drawn from four 200 gall. Tanks
   　　　at MORRISON - T.28.c.6.5. - filled nightly by Light
   　　　Railway under Water Supply Officer's arrangements.
   　　　It is filled in petrol tanks and conveyed as follows:-
   　　　　For 3 Coys by push lines to B.2.a.7.8. thence by
   　　　　　limber to Cookhouses, VANCOUVER.
   　　　　For 1 Coy and Battn. H.Q. by push lines to Battn. H.Q.
   　(b). If this supply fails water may be drawn from VIMY
   　　　Brewery - T.28.a.5.0. - from pipe-filled tanks.
   　(c). Washing water may be drawn from FARBUS WELLS.
   (iv). **T.M. Battery H.Q.** Drinking water is drawn from MERSEY.
   (v). **Brigade H.Q.** Drinking water is drawn from 400 gall.
   　　tank, filled daily by pipe.
   (vi). Petrol tins, dixies, or food containers will not be used
   　　for drawing water from wells.
   (vii). O.Cs. will ensure that each man has at least one gall. of
   　　water per day.

6. **Water Picquets.**
   (i). Water Picquets will be found by units, as per attached
   　　list which is issued to all concerned. They will report
   　　at H.Q. of the unit to be relieved at 10 a.m. on 8th July.
   (ii). Only units of the Brigade and Asb. personnel attached
   　　will be allowed to draw water from water sources in the
   　　area.
   (iii). Standing Orders for water picquets will be issued
   　　separately.

7. **AMMUNITION.**
   (i). Brigade Dumps:-
   　　LONGWOOD　...　...　B.15.a.4.8.
   　　FARBUS　...　...　B.3.d.5.1.
   　　MERSEY　...　...　B.2.c.7.7.
   　　BRICKSTACK　...　...　T.30.d.3.2.

   　　Ammunition Guards as follows will report to Sergt.
   MORRIS, Brigade Ammunition N.C.O. at Brigade H.Q. THELUS
   CAVE, at 9 a.m. on 8th instant:-
   　　4th Royal Scots　...　2 Ptes. for LONGWOOD.
   　　7th Royal Scots　...　2 Ptes. for FARBUS.
   　　7th Sco. Rifles　...　2 "　for MERSEY.
   　　7th Sco. Rifles　...　2 "　for BRICKSTACK.
   　　Transport arrangements for Ammunition Guards and Water
   Picquets will be issued later.
   (ii). **Brigade Reserve Dump.** THELUS CAVES - A.5.c.0.5.
   (iii). Except in emergency, application for Ammunition from
   　　these Dumps will be made to Brigade H.Q.

8. **R.E. MATERIAL.** /

3.

8. R.E. MATERIAL.
   (i). R.E. Officers keep in touch with C.Os. and R.E. material
        required is sent up by Light Railway from ZIVY to the
        nearest junction (LONGWOOD, MORRISON or FARBUS).
   (ii). Material for wiring should be conveyed by limber to
        VANCOUVER.

9. MEDICAL.
   (i). Right Battalion. R.A.P. - B.9.a.9.6.
        Routes of evacuation:-
            (a). Via THIRD ALLEY. Relay post at B.14.a.0.8.
            (b). Via Relay Post - B.8.d.3.4.
   (ii). Centre Battalion.)
         Left Battalion.   ) Combined R.A.P. at T.27.d.4.4.
                Evacuation to Relay Post - T.26.a.4.9.
   (iii). A.D.S. - B.2.a.9.5.
                Evacuation by push trucks to motor ambulance post -
        T.25.4.9.2., or by returning ration trucks.

10. FIRST LINE STRAGGLERS POSTS.
        Commandant's House   ...   B.7.d.5.3.
        MERSEY ALLEY   ...   ...   B.1.d.9.9.
        VIMY   ...   ...   T.25.b.5.2.

11. SALVAGE.
    Evacuation.
    (i). By returning ration limbers.
    (ii). By rail from VANCOUVER, MORRISON or FARBUS.
          Units sending salvage by (ii) will notify Brigade H.Q.
          24 hours previously.

12. BURIAL.
        Units will convey bodies to collecting station at B.2.b.2.3.
        and notify Brigade H.Q.

13. ACKNOWLEDGE.

                                              [signature]

6th July 1918.   Lieut.
                                   A/Staff Captain, 156th Inf. Brigade.

Issued at..............

==

Copy No. 1 to Brigade Commander   Copy No. 10 to 210th Coy. A.M.C.
         2   4th Royal Scots.   11   W.S.O.
         3   7th Royal Scots.   12   155th Inf. Bde.
         4   7th Scot. Rifles.   13   A.D.M.S.
         5   156th T.M. Battery   14 & 15   Diary.
         6   52nd Division.   16   File.
         7   Bde. Major.
         8   R.T.O.
         9   Bde. Sig. Officer.

==

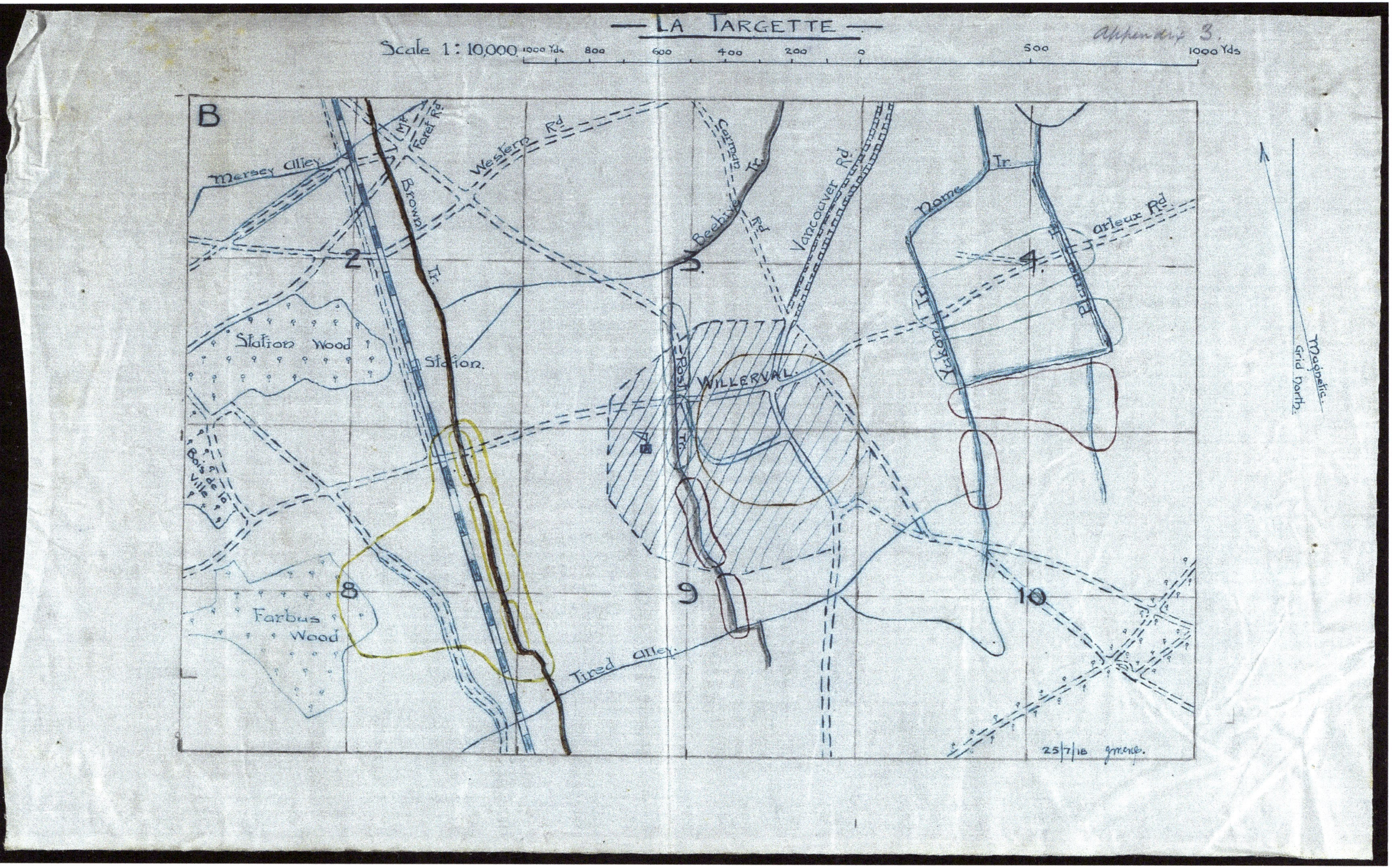
Appendix 3.
— LA TARGETTE —
Scale 1: 10,000
1000 Yds 800 600 400 200 0 500 1000 Yds
B
Mersey Alley
Mt Forêt Rd
Western Rd
Brown Tr.
Station Wood
Station.
Bois de la Ville
Farbus Wood
Tired Alley
Carman Rd
Beehive Tr.
Vancouver Rd
Post Tr.
WILLERVAL
Nome
Tr.
Yukon Tr.
Arleux Rd
2
3
4
8
9
10
Magnetic.
Grid North.
25/7/18

Operation order   Copy No 6
by
Lieut. Col. Jeff Romanes. D.S.O. Comdg   Appendix 4.
5/th Cameronians (Scottish Rifles)

Reference La TARGETTE MAP   14th July 1918.

1. 50th Canadian Battalion will take over the line from 5/th S.R. & 14th R.S. as under:—

     D. Coy. on left — Western Road - N of NOME in the Blue Line and Observation Line.
         Western Road - trench junction at B.3 central in Black Line.

     C. Coy. in Centre — From A Coys right in both lines, to O. of YUKON in Blue Line — WILLERVAL ARLEUX Road in Black Line.

     A. Coy. on Right — The remainder of all lines to present Battalion Right boundary.

     B Coy — Willerval Locality.

     Order of arrival D. C. B. A. starting to relieve about 3 p.m.

2. 44th Canadians relieve 4th R.S. and 5/th S.R. in the BROWN Line with one company each.
B Coy Canadians take over from B Coy 5/th S.R.

3. On relief Coys will proceed by Platoons to their new locations via the BROWN Line. Not more than the equivalent of a platoon at a time. 200 yards between platoons.

4. Lewis Gun Magazines. 12 drums per gun with all guns and spare parts will be man-handled. The remaining magazines will be moved by Transport after dark. Each half company in both BLUE and BLACK Lines will after relief manhandle the magazine boxes to the junction of their trench and the WILLERVAL-ARLEUX Road and form a dump by Coys at these points. Limbers will lift these after dark and convey them to near Company Headqrs. 2 men per dump will be left to load.
A Coy will make a similar dump at WILLERVAL and B Coy at the junction of BROWN LINE and the road. Coys are responsible for meeting and unloading limbers at new locations, and for guiding limbers thereto from BROWN Line — WILLERVAL Road junction.

5. <u>Rations</u> Rations will be drawn tomorrow night by Coys as under:—
     C. Coy from Morrison Dump.
     D. " " New Brunswick Dump.
     A. & B. Coys. Bordon Dump
     Headqrs by road to Headqrs.

6. **Water Arrangements.** C Coy take over Water Tins from 4th R.S. and draw from Morrison Dump.
D Coy manhandle 30 empty tins and draw from New Brunswick Dump.
A & B Coys draw 52 full tins with their rations. Each Coy will hand over 2 tins to Aid Post.
Headqrs by Water Cart at Headqrs.

7. **Advance Party.** Each Coy will send an advance party of 1 Officer and 10 men including cooks. These will carry dixies, find water and prepare evening meal for their Coys.

8. Battalion Headqrs at S.23.c.4.4 –
Aid Post at T.19.c.2.4.

9. **Signals and Runners.** C and D Coys will maintain 2 runners at 14th R.S. and 4th R.S. Headqrs respectively, at which places telephone messages will be received and despatched. B Coy will be provided with fullerphone. This will also serve A Coy.
A relay station will be established for runners at B Coy Headqrs and at S.29.d.8.9.

10. **Guides.** The following guides will report to Corporal Burke at Battn Headqrs at noon tomorrow to guide Canadian platoons. Each will carry a card with platoon number as stated.

4th S.R. No. 13   Card No. 10
  "   "   "   15   "   "   9
  "   "   "   9   "   "   4
  "   "   "   10   "   "   2
  "   "   "   11   "   "   3
  "   "   "   12   "   "   1

A Coy. 4 guides   "   " 5, 6, 7 & 8.

Dress – Runner order

French Stores Receipts for both reliefs to reach

No 1 Copy to A.C. Battn Headqrs by 12 noon on 16/4/18.
 " 2 "   " B.
 " 3 "   " C.   **Relief Complete** will be wired priority, for
 " 4 "   " D.   WILLERVAL relief by "OSCAR", for Vimy Relief
 " 5 " TO.QM by "Slater"
 " 6 "   " File
 " 7 "   " Diary
 " 8 "   "

Lieut & Adjt
1/4th Cameronians
(Scottish Rifles)

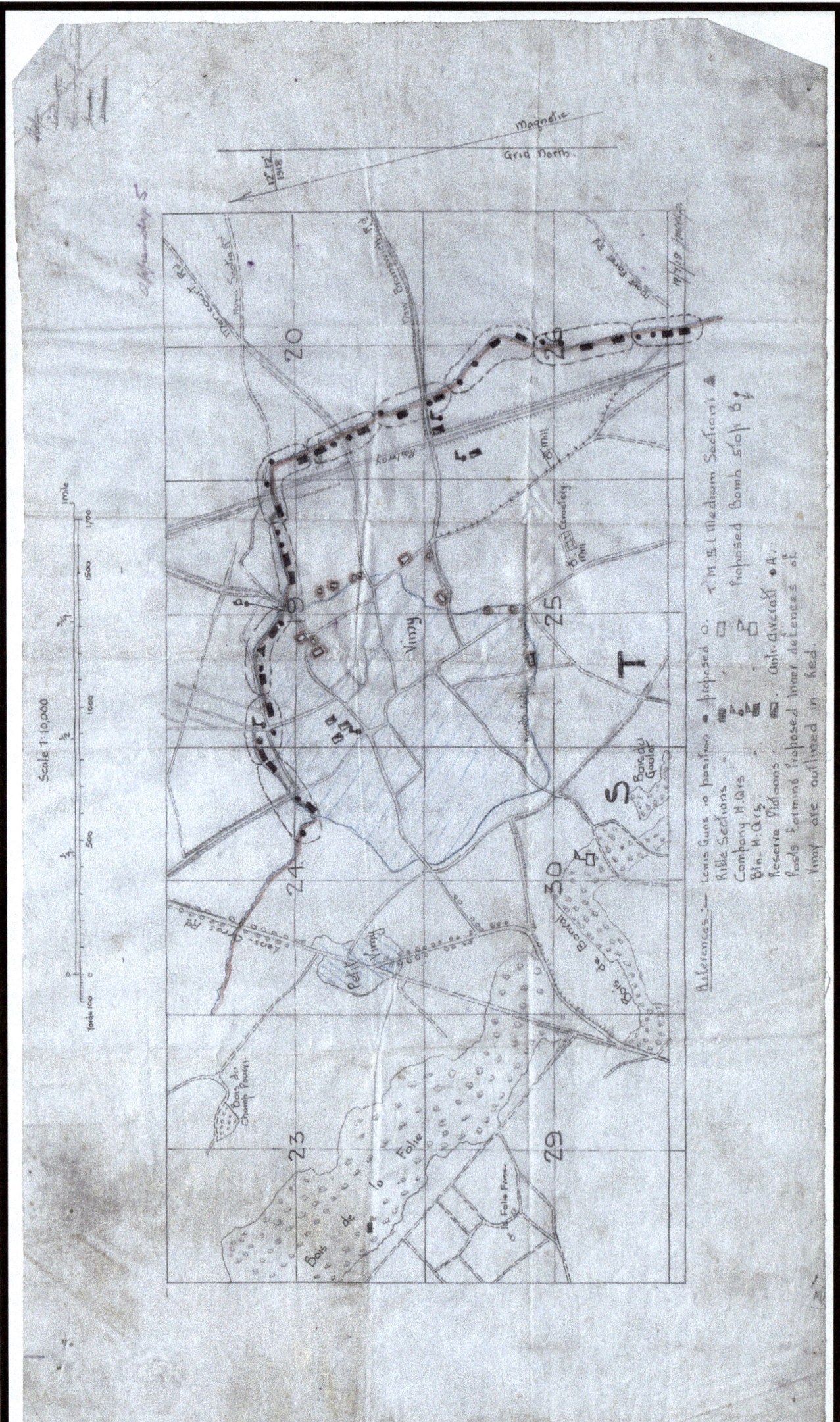

Provisional Pln Ordrs
by
Lieut. Col. J.C.P. Romanes D.S.O. Comdg.
1/7th Cameronians (Sco. Rifles)

Appendix 'C'.

20th July 1918.

1. **Intention.**
The Battalion will be relieved tomorrow, 21st inst, by the 2nd Battn. West Yorks Regt. It is not yet known what Coy of relieving Battalion will relieve 7th Cameronians Coys. Relief will commence about 4.30 p.m.

2. **Guides.**
A Chain of guides will be provided by Battn. H.Q. to entrance to PEGGIE trench. Thereafter O.C. A Coy will arrange to guide incoming Coy to D Coy and O.C. D Coy to C Coy. O.C. A Coy will arrange to divert incoming units Vimy Coy, before it reaches PEGGIE. O.C. B Coy will arrange guides for this Company.

3. **Trench Stores.**
Maps (1/10,000 & 1/20,000 only), Trench Stores, Log Books, and Lewis Gun Metal Boxes and Magazines will be handed over. An exchange of L.G. boxes has been arranged. O.C. B Coy will arrange to hand over Battn. Reserve.

4. **Move.**
After relief the Battalion will move by BROWN Line, RED TRAIL, HUMBER to S.28.d Central thence by busses to OTTAWA Camp.
Embussing Officer – 2/Lt. A.D. Hillier.
Out of trenches movement will be by platoons at 200 yards.

5. **Transport.**
One Limber per Coy will be available on night of 21st and will report at Coy H.Q. after dusk. Necessary guard and loading party will be left.

6. **Reports.**
Relief in present sector will be wired by code word "MADELAINE" and arrival in Camp by "SMITH".

Graham Allen
Lieut & Adjt.
1/7th Cameronians
(Scottish Rifles)

Operation Orders   Appendix 7
by
Lieut Colonel J. P. Pomar, D.S.O. Comg
1/5th Cameronians (Scottish Rifles)

Reference French Sheet 36.B. 1/40,000   21st July 1917.

1. Battalion will move tomorrow, 22nd inst., to Camp in vicinity of BOIS D'OLHAIN.

2. Battalion will move off at 11 a.m. after inspection by Corps Commander.

3. Dress: Fighting order.

4. Greatcoats will be tightly rolled in bundles of ten and dumped near road immediately below Q.M. Stores ready for loading by 8.30 a.m.

5. Officers Kits and Mess Stores will be dumped as in para 4 by 8.30 a.m.

6. O.C. 'B' Coy will detail two platoons to report to Q.M. at 8.30 a.m. to load Greatcoats and Kits as detailed above. This party will also load all Battalion Limbers except Lewis Gun Limbers.

7. Coys will be responsible for the loading of their own Lewis Gun limber. Coy Lewis Gunners should be detailed for this purpose.

8. The loading party referred to in para 6, or such of them as may be detailed by Q.M. will proceed on the motor lorries and will unload on arrival at new camp.

9. Q.M. will arrange for the loading of Packs at LATTA Camp at 8.30 a.m.

10. Transport will march in rear of Battalion. O.C. B Coy will detail their A.A. Lewis Gun teams to accompany Transport. N.C.O's i/c will report to T.O. at 9.45 a.m.

11. The following distances will be maintained en route:-
    Between Coys – 100 yards.
    Battalion and Transport – 100 yards.

12. Water Bottles will be filled immediately after breakfast and no water will be drunk thereafter without permission of an Officer.

2.

13. O.C. Coys will ensure that lines is left scrupulously clean and tidy.
14. Breakfast will be at 7.30 am. The mens Messing Hut will not be used for this Meal.
15. Coys will render a Marching-out state to O.R. by 8.30 am. This state will shew (1) Number actually marching with Coy. (2) Personnel proceeding with Transport (3) Personnel who have proceeded in advance. (4) Any other details, and will include Battn. HQ personnel.
16. Waterproof sheets will be rolled in bundles of 10 and will be handed in with Greatcoats as in para 4.

Capt & adjt.
4th Cameronians
(Sco Rifles)

Appendix 7A.

Until further orders the Brigade is in G.H.Q. Reserve and will be ready to move by tactical train or bus at 4 hours notice.

On receipt of orders to move Coys will parade in their own lines. Lewis Guns and spare parts will be loaded by Coy Lewis Gunners on limbers which will arrive at EASTERN entrance to the camp.

Every available man will parade in full marching order. Steel Helmets will be worn and P. or P. Respirators carried slung.

A.A. Lewis Gunners will march to embussing or entraining points with the limbers, and during march will be ready to use their guns if required.

Coys will report immediately they are ready to move. Separate orders have been issued to T.O. as to number of animals and vehicles to proceed.

Before leaving every man will be issued with one complete days rations.

<u>Move by bus.</u> Brigade will rendezvous at J.36.a.11. Battalion route to that point will be :-

Along track from Q.14.b.1.6 to Q.Y.d.5.9. thence to Q.Y.d.3.8. and along track through Q.Y. Central Q.1.c.0.0. Q.6. Central to J.36.a.11.

Time allowed 1 hour and 15 minutes.

<u>Move by train.</u> Brigade will rendezvous at P.10.b.0.8. Battalion route to that point will be :-

Along road from Q.14.b.1.6 through Q.14.c.0.1. to road junction at Q.19.a.1.2. Thence along road N.W. through OLHAIN, BARAFFLE to P.10.b.0.8.

Time allowed 1 hour and 20 minutes.

(Sgd) C.S. Romanes Lt. Col.
Comdg. 1/4th Cameronians
(Sco. Rifles)

1/4th Cameronians (Scottish Rifles)

Training Programme.

Appendix 8

Hour	Thursday 25th July	Friday 26th July	Saturday 27th July	Sunday 28th July	Tuesday 29th July	Friday 30th July
8.30 to 9.30	March to Parade Ground.	Route Marches	As for Thursday 25th	As for Thursday 25th	As for Thursday 25th	As for Friday 26th
9.30 to 11.00	Tactical Exercises for Platoons	Lewis Gun training. Musketry.				
11.00 to 11.30	Coy. Close Order Drill.	Handling of Arms. Lectures.	Range Practices.	Thursday 25th	Thursday 25th	Friday 26th Range Practices.
11.30 to 12.30.	March to Camp.					

Signallers daily under the Signalling Officer.
Scouts   "   "   "   "   Scout   "
Lewis Gun classes for Officers and N.C.O's daily from 2.30 to 3.30.
Junior N.C.O's daily from 3-4. under R.S.M.

24/7/18

Lt. Colonel.
Comdg. 1/4th Cameronians
(Sco. Rifles)

Operation Orders
by
Lieut. Col. G. N. Romanes, D.S.O.
Comdg. 9th The Cameronians (Sco. Rifles)

Appendix 9.
Copy No. 9.

29th July 1916

1. Battalion will move tomorrow to ECOIVRES area.
2. Coys. will be paraded in their lines ready to move off at 8-50 a.m.
3. Officers kits and stores will be dumped at Q.M. store by 7-30 a.m.
4. Packs, which will contain greatcoats and waterproof sheets will be dumped at eastern edge of camp by 7 a.m.
5. O.C. "D" Coy. will supply a loading party of 1 platoon to report to Q.M. Store to load the G.S. wagons at 7.45 a.m; and a party of 2 sections to load motor lorries under superintendence of Asst. Adjt. at 7.15 a.m.
6. Coys. will march at 100 yards distance and transport will follow 100 yards in rear of "A" Coy.
7. Order of March - H.Q., "D", "C", "B", "A".
8. Camps will be left scrupulously clean.
9. Strict march discipline must be maintained & no man is to fall out or drink from his water-bottle without permission of an Officer.
10. Water-bottles will be filled by 8 a.m.
11. Asst. Adjt. will obtain a certificate as to cleanliness of area from Area Commdt.
12. Tea will be ready for troops on arrival at new area.

(Sd) Hector E. Maclean
Capt. & Adjt.
9th The Cameronians
(Sco. Rifles)

Distribution:
"A" Coy - Copy No. 1
"B" "   "   " 2
"C" "   "   " 3
"D" "   "   " 4
Q.M.   "   " 5
T.O.   "   " 6
H.Q.   "   " 7
FILE   "   " 8 & 9

Army Form C. 2118.

WAR DIARY
or
INTELLIGENCE SUMMARY.
(Erase heading not required.)

Vol 5

1/4th Cameronians (-S.R)

WAR DIARY
for
AUGUST 1918

VOLUME XXXIX

Reference Maps LENS - 1/10,000
+ attached tracing

WAR DIARY
or
INTELLIGENCE SUMMARY.
(Erase heading not required.)

Army Form C. 2118.

A.(1)

August 1918.

Place	Date	Hour	Summary of Events and Information	Remarks and references to Appendices
GAVRELLE.	1st		The Battalion took over yesterday from the 54th Canadian Bn.. for dispositions see appendix I	appx I
	2nd		A quiet day. Weather showery. No patrols allowed beyond advanced nights positions until further orders.	
	3rd		Weather bright but showery. Enemy artillery quiet.	
	4th		The Battalion took over new positions slightly to the left (see appendices II + III)	appendices II + III
	5th		Day O.P. established in No MANS LAND. No enemy movements detected. Quiet day.	
	6th		Our artillery very active during the day + nights 6th/7th. Enemy artillery normal.	
	7th		Weather today was showery. Very quiet day.	
	8th		Nothing of interest happened. Weather dry + clear.	
	9th		Enemy artillery was fairly active during the day but otherwise nothing to report.	
	10th		Quiet day. Weather continued fine.	
	11th		- do -	
	12th		Quiet day. At night 2/Lt. Ross + 2 Rifle Sections patrolled No MANS LAND. No enemy was encountered.	
	13th		Very quiet day.	

Rhee H.Q. LENS WAR DIARY
1/20000
or
INTELLIGENCE SUMMARY.
(Erase heading not required.)
August 1918.

Army Form C. 2118.
A.3

Place	Date	Hour	Summary of Events and Information	Remarks and references to Appendices
	13th		At night a patrol of 2 Officers (Lt. Maclaurin, 2/Lt. R Glass) + 2 Rifle Sections patrolled No MANS LAND + enemy wire. No enemy were met.	~~~~
	14th		2/Lt. Season + 2 Rifle Sections patrolled No MANS LAND. No enemy encountered. Quiet day.	~~~~
SAVY.	15th 16th		In the evening the Bttn. was relieved (appendix) by the 4th. Seaforths (51st. Division) + on relief marched to ECURIE LIGHT RLY. STN. (Lens map 1/100,000) + entrained for SAVY. (Lens Map 1/100,000) where Battn. is now billetted. The day was spent in resting + cleaning up.	appx 1& 2 ~~~~
	17th		The day was spent bathing + cleaning up.	~~~~
	18th		Training commenced today (appx.) A report of damage to a Lewis Gun is appended.	~~~~
	19th		Training carried out as per programme.	~~~~
	20th		- Do -	~~~~
	21st		In the evening orders were received for the Battn. to move (appx.) Battn. left SAVY at 11.45 P.M. + marched to WARLUS (Lens Map 1/100,000) where accommodated in huts.	~~~~
WARLUS.	21st		The day was spent resting.	~~~~
	22nd		Orders were received for the Battn. to proceed by Buss to BLAIRVILLE (Lens Map 1/100,000) The Battn. was ready to move at 2.45 P.M. By 5 P.M. only 8 Busses had arrived. All Lewis Gunners + their equipment were sent forward in advance.	~~~~

Reference Map 51^b S.W. 1:20.000 (App VII)
LENS 1:100.000

Army Form C. 2118.

WAR DIARY
or
INTELLIGENCE SUMMARY.
(Erase heading not required)

A 4.

August 1918

Place	Date	Hour	Summary of Events and Information	Remarks and references to Appendices
WARLUS.	22nd		While in billets an order was received by the Commanding Officer to report to Brigade Headquarters by 9 a.m. with four other Officers. Warning orders were received at the same time to prepare to move. A Divisional Conference was held at Adainville Quarries. This was the first indication that an attack was in contemplation. After the Divisional Conference was concluded a short Brigade Conference was held & a hasty order the Brigadier other Officers went little or no time to reconnoitre the first line. As the attack was to take place early the following morning there was little or no time for conference of instructions were given that probably the Brigade would attack on a three Battalion front the 7th S.R. on the left, 6th 7th Royal Scots in the centre & the 4th 5th Royal Scots on the right. It was also known that three tanks would co-operate. What reconnaissance was possible was completed about 4 p.m. & at 8 p.m. a second Brigade Conference was held at which orders were finally dictated in Cafe in reserve. Here final instructions were given the C.O.'s. It was written that the railway cutting behind the first lines. Meanwhile the Battalion & the transport had been moved up by bus to BRETONCOURT & these were to move again by bus close behind the first lines three march to their points of assembly. Owing to the breakdown in transport arrangements at BRETONCOURT the Battalion only began to arrive at about 10 o'clock & were not completely at the assembly points till well after 2 a.m. Having had no hot meal since breakfast time the Quartermaster had arranged for tea & turn to come to the Battalion at the points of assembly but owing to congestion of roads, the cookers limbers were unable to come up. The orders for assault were as previously described. The objective of the Battalion being the enemy first system between Stargap & corner of Hamon Trench inclusive. Zero hour was to be 4.55 a.m. when a barrage would fall on Enemy Lines three 12 minutes the tanks were to catch up with the infantry from their points of assembly & at zero +12 the whole line was to advance.	LENS 1/100.000 LENS 1/100.000 51 B.S.W. M.30+36
In the field	23rd		Guides were provided by the Royal Sussex Regt. who were killing the line to guide platoons on to the tape which had been laid by the Royal Engineers in front of our first wire. Tape had been cut struck ridges had been laid. Unfortunately heavy enemy gas shelling as well as a certain amount of H.E. caused the guides to take to the Trenches instead of skirting overland as had been agreed, in consequence there was much cross traffic, the effect of which was that the Battalion was delayed in getting on to the tape, the final men reaching it a few minutes only before zero hour. The order of battle was as follows. "C" Coy on the right in touch with 7th Royal Scots "D" Coy on the left, with "A" Coy. & "B" Coy. & D.B. Coy in support of D.B. Coy.	

Reference Map
5/ B.S.W. 10000

Army Form C. 2118.

A 5.

WAR DIARY
or
INTELLIGENCE SUMMARY.
(Erase heading not required.)

Place	Date	Hour	Summary of Events and Information	Remarks and references to Appendices
In the field	23		The objective was divided equally between the leading Companies. Battalion Headquarters were established in the front line at the road junction of Sans Honore, in touch with Brigade Headquarters by telephone. Every assistance had been afforded by the Royal Sussex Regt. informing the Battalion of for the assault. From zero hour a heavy barrage was put down on our objective & at Zero +12 the troops moved off under the Barrage little opposition was met with during the taking of the objective which was taken without the assistance of the tanks which there late, & only passed through our line after the objective had been achieved. As soon as the objective was nearly reached, two platoons of "C" Coy dealt with it taking 4 prisoners + a light gun + Lewis guns were brought into play against about 30 Germans who were retiring from this point + accounted for most of them. "D.C" Coy came under a certain amount of machine gun fire but this was speedily wiped out, Dr "D" Coy as did "C" Coy came under fairly heavy barrage of 5.95 + minenwerfs, but achieved their objective (Dogsap) with few casualties. Nos 13 + 15 Platoons who formed the first wave cleared Dogsap with little opposition + a number of the enemy who were nothing were brought down by Lewis gun + rifle fire. At this juncture. At number of dugouts were found + bombed a few men prisoners being taken straight forward to exploit successes. No 15 Platoon worked at this point Nos 13 + 15 Platoons pressed No 13 Platoon was held up for a short time by a machine gun but the crew of which soon surrendered on being turned on with flanks. Second Lieut S Glass was wounded at this time No.15 Platoon established a bombing block in the trench at N.31.a.2.8. Second Lieutenant Watson (Platoon Commander) with a small party patrolled northward for 300 yards, capturing 3 officers and some prisoners + 2 machine guns. Consolidation was proceeded with all objectives were in hand by 6.15 a.m. During consolidation Second Lieutenant Watson pressed forward by himself + succeeded in capturing a machine gun with a crew of four. Its crew so consolidation was within hand 2 N.C. + P. Companies were themselves + held positions in depth according to plan. Fairly harassing fire from artillery trench mortars was kept up on our front line, the whole coming from the direction of Hinity Structure. At 6.30 P.M. "D" Coy. sent out 2 patrols one towards Trinity Structure + one to the Map, the first to test the strength of the enemy the second the double object of seeing whether the trench between our left & the road was occupied by the enemy + secondly to keep in touch with the Canadians. By some error the division had been informed that the Canadians were occupying this trench also Henin Trench at N.35.b.(?) + considerable difficulty was experienced in ensuring them that this was not the fact. On the contrary HENIN Trench at N.35.d.4.2. was found to be strongly held by	6 N.25. um

Reference Map
51 b S.W. 1/20000

WAR DIARY
or
INTELLIGENCE SUMMARY.

A.6.

August 1918

Army Form C. 2118.

Place	Date	Hour	Summary of Events and Information	Remarks and references to Appendices
In the field	24		the enemy who had also minunen established in Fritz Structure. The trench leading to the Mage was found to be empty, the Mage itself being occupied by Canadians. Lieutenant Gordon did good work with the patrol to Fritz Structure & brought back valuable information. At 2 A.M. the Brigadier arrived at Battalion Headquarters with a warning order for an attack whose zero hour was to be 7 A.M. The final objective being the sunken road running through N.26. Central, the frontage allotted to the Battalion being from N.26.g.6.0. to N.26. Central. 7th Royal Scots on our right & the Canadians on our left. He warned the C.O. at the time that though latence of divisional orders it would probably be impossible to get written orders to reach the battalion before zero hour. D.B. Coy was moved into the trench running towards the Mage in order that at zero hour its right coy, the advance of the remainder of the battalion. This coy having to patrol & carrying parties was much scattered & had considerable time to collect them & move them into their position. Owing to darkness and ignorance of the ground the trench allotted to them was occupied without being noticed. The position was taken up by the Company commander of the Sunken Road running through N.25.c. Here it was discovered by the Company Commander to be late to retiring at 6.20 A.M. B. M. 9.11 (Appendix F) was received. It was too late to then verbal instructions as to their role & their objective. The Scout Officer to the left companies to give them verbal instructions as to their role & their objective. Owing to war diction great difficulty was experienced by the Scout Officer in finding D.B. Coy. In spite of these difficulties objectives were reached without difficulty resistance being practically Nil. The line was now held by A. Coy on the right in touch with 7th R.S., C. Coy in the Ctr, R.B., & D. Coy. in support. As no touch had been established with the Canadians the guarding of the left flank was entrusted to D. Coy, whose O.C. made the necessary dispositions. As a very considerable number of machine guns were at the disposal of the C.O. this flank was able to be strongly guarded, until such time as the Canadians should make necessary adjustment. During the afternoon instructions were received to push out patrols to the Hindenburg line to ascertain if it was held by the enemy. These patrols were sent out by A. & D. Coys. were in both cases met by heavy machine gun fire & sustained casualties. All patrols were, however, well handled, & were able to return to give useful information as to location of enemy machine guns. Patrol leaders were 266065 Sgt. Lilte K. 265418 L/Cpl Stewart J. Towards evening Canadians adjusted their line & obtained touch with our left thus enabling D. Coy to	7

WAR DIARY or INTELLIGENCE SUMMARY

Army Form C. 2118.

Reference Map 51B S.W. 2.0.0.0

August 1918

A.Y.

Place	Date	Hour	Summary of Events and Information	Remarks and references to Appendices
In the field	25		be relieved of its duties as protector of the flank. At 8 p.m. B.M. 157 (Appendix 2) was received fixing the divisional northern boundary so that a results the battalion boundary was the grid line dividing N.19 & N.25. The necessary adjustment was made by D. Coy. taking over the left of the line with C. in the centre & A on the right each Coy. with 2 platoons in the line & 2 in support B. Coy. remaining in support. No centrale Battalion Headquarters had been established at N.25.0.3.3. About 9.30 p.m. an order was received to the effect that no part of our line was to be within 500 yds of the enemy line (B.M. 162 - Appendix 2) & that this would consequently involve moving back from N.26. Central to N.25. a.8.9. where a junction would be effected with the Canadians. This involved a further move by C. & D. Coys & it by 11.30 p.m. the C.O. was able to report to Brigade that the line was completely readjusted.	
	26		At 1.30 A.M. B.M.148 (Appendix) was received intimating that the 155 Brigade would attack at 3 a.m. & during instruction as to the guarding of the assembly troops. Guides had previously been sent out to await instructions having been requested but unfortunately were not picked up by assaulting Battalion which did not reach Battalion H.Q. until after 2 A.M. From Battalion H.Q. they were guided to their jumping off grounds while they were only able to reach at here by very great efforts. O.C. B. Coy. differentiable troubles in arranging guides & giving information for these troops. The attack by 155 Bde. bore completed successful & all objectives were gained. About 11 A.M. orders were received for the Battalion to more forward to support 155 Bde. in Hindenburg Line this was done, but not before 4 p.m. before the final dispositions of the Battalion had been rattled orders were received (B.M. 202-Appendix 5) to concentrate Battalion at N.27.b. The C.O. received personal instructions from B.G.C. to more Battalion to T.6.a. where it would be in reserve to 156 Brigade. At 9 p.m. concentration was complete & Battalion moved off to arriving at N.28.c.7.4. Information was received from 156. Brigade Major that T.6.a. was still in hands of the enemy & that to more there now be attended by difficulties. The Battalion therefore remained for the night in the Hindenburg Line between N.28.c.7.5. & N.28.c.7.0. Bde. being notified accordingly. Considerable gas shelling was experienced during the night, but no casualties resulted.	
	27		About 9 A.M. the 27th verbal orders were received by C.O. from B.G.C. that Brigade would advance on FONTAINE LES CROSSELLES at 10 A.M. the Battalion being in support. This operation was in conjunction with an advance on Rieucourt by 154th Inf. Bde. & on CHERISY by Canadian Division.	

D. D. & L., London, E.C.
Wt W177/M2031 750,000 5/17 Sch. 83 Forms/C2118/14

Reference Map
51 B.S.W. NoseO

WAR DIARY
or
INTELLIGENCE SUMMARY.
(Erase heading not required.)

Army Form C. 2118.

August 1918.   A 8

Place	Date	Hour	Summary of Events and Information	Remarks and references to Appendices
In the field	28th 29th 30th 31st		At 10 P.M. "A" & "B" Coys were moved forward to CROW TRENCH to be ready to advance in rear of the Royal Scots Battalions "C" & "D" Coys remaining as before at midday these 2 Coys advanced into close support of Royal Scots Battalions which had now reached the line of the RIVER SENSÉE C & D/ Coys & Battalion Headquarters moved further up. Battalion H.Q. being established (together with Bde H.Q.) in FIRST AVENUE (O.31.c.0.7.) No further advance was made by Brigade which was relieved by Canadian Division at night & moved back to Divisional area at our original front line near ROSS TRENCH. Day spent in resting & taking deficiency stats of fighting kit. Weather showery. — So — Clean clothing issued. Battalion gathering Salvage. Weather dry. Battalion moved up to support line relieving Battalion of 56th Division between CROISELLES and ECOUST.	appx VI

Casualties – Officers.
Other Ranks.

	Killed	Wounded.	Missing.
	—	2	1 remained at duty.
	10	88.	4
		3 accidental	4 remaining at duty.
		41 to Hospital. Gas.	

E.P. Murray Lt Col

A(1)

Strength in the field – 31st July, 1918
to 31st August, 1918

	O	OR
	30	8852
	28	6226
Decrease	2	226

	O	OR
Increase		
Reinforcements	0	—
From Hospital	5	5
Detachment T	1	40
Other Causes	12	193
	18	238
Decrease		
To Hospital	2	125
Killed	—	12
Wounded	2	102
Missing	—	4
Courts	6	18
Leave	4	111
Other Causes	6	72
	20	444

Officers

Increase
Lt Souter James
Lt J Haydock "
2/Lt Bird "
" Eyckert "
" Brown "
Lt A Dunlop from course
Lieut Anderson "
2/Lt Maclachlan "
Lt C Allis "
M/Lt Cullen "
Capt Walker from leave
" Wilson "
Lt C Gray "
Lieut Anderson "
Lt. C. Ellies from Hospital
Lt Kerr "
M/Lt Morrison "
Lt Kerr "

Decrease
2/Lt Auchterlonie To leave
2/Lt Cullen "
Lt Johnson "
2/Lt Brooks "
Macallin "
Lt A Forbes "
Lieut Anderson To leave
Captain Aitken "
Captain Ryther To her Camp
Lt A Bird To 15th Div
2/Lt Strathearn To Stn
2/Lt Stokes " "
Lt Kerr To Hospital Sh
Macklau Wounded
" F! Dunn "
" McAllister "
" A Silva "
to Permanenth Airgoss
Lt Morrillion Rest Camp
2/Lt Kerr Specialist RS
To UK
To R.F.F.
To 15th Bys
To Offring Cadet B
To Inst Course

APP. I

— DISPOSITION SKETCH —

REF. MAP POINT DU JOUR.

1:10,000

1/7TH CAMERONIANS (SCO. RIF.)

REFERENCE:—
- Bn. H.Q.
- Coy. H.Q.
- Lewis Guns
- Rifle Sect.
- Block. B
- Btn. O.P.
- Machine Gun. M.G.
- Aid Post.

Operation Orders

Appendix II

by

Lt. Col. J. G. P. Romanes D.S.O.
Comdg. Bn. The Cameronians (Sco Rifles)

5th August 1918

1. The following moves and reliefs will be carried out tomorrow, 6th inst, on re-adjustment of Battalion boundaries.

2. Final Location of Coys will be:—

"A" Coy - POST LINE - (KAY ALLEY inclusive to B.28.a.y.3.
1 platoon in POST SUPPORT.
Admin H.Q. at 'B' Coy. present H.Q.
Battle H.Q. in POST SUPPORT Line.

"B" Coy - FRONT LINE - (B.28.d.9.9. - B.23.c.6.0.)
H.Q. at STERLING POST.

"C" Coy - FRONT LINE - (THAMES ALLEY excl. but including dug-outs to B.28.d.9.9.
H.Q. at "A" Coy. present H.Q.

"D" Coy - POST LINE - (H.3.b.8.2. to KAY ALLEY exclusive)
H.Q. at 'B' Coy present H.Q.

3. Moves

"D" Coy. on relief via THAMES and TOWY.
"C" Coy. (MACK and LEFT platoons) - do -
"C" Coy (REMAINDER) via MISSOURI and KAY
"A" Coy. via BAILLEUL ALLEY.
"B" Coy. ———— do ————

In all cases, precedence will be given to troops moving up to front line.

4. Relieving Units

"D" Coy. will be relieved by 2/5th S. LANCS.
"C" Coy (MACK platoon) ——— do ———
"C" Coy (2 platoons) by 1st R.M.F.
"C" Coy (left platoon) by "D" Coy.
"A" Coy. by "C" Coy
"B" Coy. by "D" and "A" Coys.

5. From tomorrow night (6th inst) rations for all Coys. will be drawn at B.27.a.1.4., and water for all Coys at B.27.a.0.4.
"B" and "C" Coys. will provide carrying parties for front line Coys. Further instructions will be issued later.

6. Advance parties of 1 Officer per Coy and 1 N.C.O. per platoon should proceed to new areas as soon as possible tomorrow morning to take over stores, etc.

Receipt/

6.(Contd) Receipts for all trench stores taken or handed over to reach Orderly Room by 9 a.m. on 4th inst.

7. Move will take place in afternoon and will be completed by 6 p.m.

8. Completion to be notified by code word "REALLY."

9. Aid Post will move to dug-out at junction of POST LANE and TOWY ALLEY.

9. Lewis Gun Magazines may be exchanged within the Battalion by arrangement.

10. Battn. H.Q. remain at present location.

(Sgd) Hector C Maclean
Captain
Ca The Cameronians
(Sco. Rifles)

Appendix III

Appendix IV

Operation Orders
by
Lieut. Col. L.F.E. Lemans D.S.O.
Comdg 2nd The Cameronians (Sco. Rifles)

15th Aug 1916

1. **Relief.** Battalion will be relieved by 10th Seaforths to-night, 15/16th and on relief will move back to an area to be defined later. Guides for relieving troops on the scale of 1 per platoon and 1 per Coy H.Q. will report at Battalion H.Q. at 4.30 p.m. to-day prompt.

2. All maps, log books, communications map, and photographic plans of projected operations trench stores, work traces, etc., will be handed over and receipts obtained and forwarded to Battalion Orderly Room by mid-day on 16th inst. Companies will move back via RAY and TONY ALLEY.

3. **Lewis Guns.** Coy L.G. Limbers will be at Battalion Headquarters ready on these will be loaded all magazines and guns. Coy L.G. N.C.O. will report to Battalion Lewis Gun Officer by 6 p.m. to arrange details of loading.

4. **Completion of Relief.** Completion of relief will be reported by wire to Major General.

Capt & Adjt

Operation Order
by
Lieut-Col J.G.P. Romanes, DSO
Comdg. Bn. The Cameronians (Sco Rifles)

15th August 1918

1. After relief by 4th Seaforths tonight coys will move by platoons to ECURIE Light Railway Station (A.20.t.9.1) The following will be the route:-
   Battalion Headquarters - TOWY TRACK -
   Bailleul Road - Artillery Track B -
   Lawrence Avenue - main road through
   ROCLINCOURT - ECURIE - MADAGASCAR CORNER
   to ECURIE Light Railway Station.

2. Platoons must keep together, and no straggling or falling out permitted under any circumstances whatsoever.

3. Scout Officer will post scouts at road junctions to point out to coys the proper road. These scouts will be picked up by the last party.

4. 16 Magazines per Lewis Gun will be carried by personnel. The remaining magazines will be sent down with 2 men per coy and will be loaded on train under Battalion arrangements. These two men will proceed with this train and they will report to Battalion Lewis Gun Officer at 7 p.m.

5. Divis and cook-house stores may also be sent down to be loaded on this train but must be at Battalion Headquarters by 7 p.m. at latest.

6. Battalion will assemble at ECURIE Light Railway Station and will entrain there. Battalion Entraining Officer - Capt. Mather who will choose a suitable assembly spot, and will arrange the allotment of train accommodation.

7. Battalion will detrain at SAVY Station. Battalion Detraining Officer - Lieut. D. McWilliam

8. Battalion will billet in the villages of SAVY and BERLETTE until further orders. Immediately after arrival coys will mount their Anti-Aircraft Lewis Guns under the direction of Battalion Lewis Gun Officer.

9. Except where amended, previous Operation Orders hold good.

10. All Lewis Gun magazines will be carried by personnel.

15/8/18

[signature]
Capt. & Adjt.

Lt McLauren
Lt Dunlop
Lt Hillyer

Operation Orders
by
Lieut Col. J.G.R. Romanes, D.S.O.
Comdg. Bn. The Cameronians (Scot Rifles)

Appx VI

31st August 1918

1. **Relief** — The Brigade will relieve 167 Inf. Bde. tonight.
2. **Move** — Battalion will move off from this camp at 4-30 p.m. Order of march "C", "D", "A", "B", Battn. H.Q., Transport. Platoons will march at 100 yards distance.
3. Brigade is concentrating at T.4.c.4.4. at which point a hot meal will be issued. This will be cooked on the cookers en route under arrangements to be made by Q.M.
3. **Kits** — All Officers kits & stores will be dumped at Q.M. Stores by 2-30 p.m.
4. **Lewis Guns.** All Lewis Guns and magazines will be loaded on limbers by 3-30 p.m. These will be drawn by Coys. at T.4.c.4.4. and guns and 12 magazines per gun manhandled from that point forward. 40 magazines per Coy. will be carried throughout on pack ponies. Transport Officer will arrange accordingly.
5. **Rations.** Rations for 1st prox will be carried on the man. Water bottles will be carried full.
6. **Completion of Relief.** Relief complete will be notified to Battalion Headquarters by code word "CAPT MACLAURIN".
7. **Nucleus.** Nucleus will move under Major Masher to whom orders will be issued.

Capt & Adjt
Bn The Cameronians
(Scot Rifles)

Vol 6

4 copies

1/7th CAMERONIANS
(Scottish Rifles)
SEPTEMBER 1918
VOL 40.

Army Form C. 2118.

WAR DIARY
or
INTELLIGENCE SUMMARY.
(Erase heading not required.)

MAP REFERENCE.
51b S.W. S.7c N.E.   G.(2).

SEPTEMBER

Place	Date SEPT	Hour	Summary of Events and Information	Remarks and references to Appendices
T 24 d 75	1		156. Inf. Bde. in support to 155 Inf. Bde. Orders were received in the morning that 156 Bde. would probably attack through 155. Bde. Objective HINDENBURG SYSTEM west of QUEANT. These orders were eventually cancelled.	
		6.30 pm	Battalion H.Q. moved from T 24 d 75 to T U 20 c 26	App. I
		9.00 pm	Orders received for attack on 2nd Inf Brigade Operation order No 54	App. II
	2	4.45 am	Battalion in position in TANK SUPPORT U 28 b & d. A considerable amount of gas experienced. Diary of Operations Sept 1st 3rd	
		8.00 am	Verbal telephone message received from Brigade that zero hour would be 8.45 am.	
		8.10 am	Battalion moved out to jumping off position.	
		8.45 am	Barrage came down, which was both weak and inaccurate. 'C' Coy. suffering several casualties from it.	
		9.40 am	'B' and 'C' Coys held up by wire in front of HINDENBURG LINE, which had been untouched by barrage.	

Army Form C. 2118.

MAP REF. 51 b SW
57 c NE 57 c NW 51 b SE

WAR DIARY
or
INTELLIGENCE SUMMARY.
(Erase heading not required.)

A 3

Instructions regarding War Diaries and Intelligence Summaries are contained in F. S. Regs., Part II. and the Staff Manual respectively. Title pages will be prepared in manuscript.

Place	Date	Hour	Summary of Events and Information	Remarks and references to Appendices
	2 Sept (cont)	10.30 am	1 Section "C" Coy (C/L. STAG) succeeded in entering HINDENBURG LINE and accounted for 13 Germans before being compelled to withdraw on arrival of enemy reinforcements. Both flanks of the battalion were at this time unprotected. 4th Royal Scots came up on left flank. Enemy made several attempts at outflanking from Railway Line C 5 d and C 6 c. These attempts frustrated by D Coy. and Machine Guns on right flank. Position maintained in front of our line for 5½ hours, in spite of heavy M.G. fire. Several attempts were made during this time to effect an entry into trench, but without success. Two enemy M.G.s were taken on and knocked out by Lewis guns. All communication between Coys and Battalion H.Q. was by runners, who had to cross the spur invariably under heavy fire.	
		3.30 pm	Hostile M.G. fire decreased, and scouts reported HINDENBURG LINE evacuated. "B" and "C" Coys pushed forward and occupied trenches. Battalion immediately advanced to final objective, again under heavy M.G. fire from QUEANT. "D" Coys Lewis guns engaged hostile M.Gs. in QUEANT which were silenced, and casualties seem to be inflicted on the teams. This allowed the battalion to reach its final objective (6.10 pm.) SUNKEN ROAD in D.1.a. to cross roads D.1.b. Three north-west to cross-roads V 25 c. At this line QUEANT was still strongly held by the enemy.	

Army Form C. 2118.

MAP REF.
51 b SW 57 c NE 57 c NW

WAR DIARY
or
INTELLIGENCE SUMMARY.
(Erase heading not required)

A(4).

Instructions regarding War Diaries and Intelligence Summaries are contained in F. S. Regs., Part II. and the Staff Manual respectively. Title pages will be prepared in manuscript.

Place	Date Sept	Hour	Summary of Events and Information	Remarks and references to Appendices
	2 (cont.)	9.30 p.m.	Very light and M.G. in QUEANT cease, and patrols pushing forward, reported the town evacuated. Patrolling was continued throughout the night.	AJU
U 30 d	3	7.45 a.m.	Patrol to PRONVILLE reported town evacuated.	
		8.30 a.m.	On 155 Bde passing through to occupy HINDENBURG LINE East and South of QUEANT, 156 Bde concentrated in U 30 d.	
			Casualties during this operation (1st - 3rd Sept) were 7 officers wounded. O.R. Killed 11, wounded 54. Captures included 7 M.G. and 3 trench mortars. In the afternoon the Bde. was visited by Mr HARRY LAUDER.	
	4		Day spent resting and collecting salvage.	AJU
	5		Orders were received that Division would be relieved by 56th Div. to night. At 7 p.m. orders were later cancelled.	AJU
	6		Work of collecting salvage carried on.	AJU
	7	7 a.m.	The Division being relieved, Battalion moved to Buissu area.	AJU
B 2 d 27	8		B 2 c and d near ST LEGER. Batn. arrived in new area at 11 a.m. Nucleus formed S. McGILCHRIST reported for duty, Lt/Col G. ACQ Mc HERD and BROWN Church Parade 10 a.m. Salvage work carried on after this parade the MgGregor pipers, 51st Div. Pipe Band, walking Officers during the afternoon. 2/Lt Anderson Hopewell O/c Pow Guy walking Officers.	AJU

MAP REF.
57c NW

Place: B 2 d 2.7

Date Sept.	Hour	Summary of Events and Information	Remarks and references to Appendices
9		Inspection of Bde by Sir Charles Fergusson Bt. KCB KCMG MVO ? the Corps Commander, cancelled owing to very heavy rain. The following were awarded the Military Medal for conduct in recent operations. 26605 A/Cpl L. Lobb. 200553 Pte. H. McKinnon. 34628 Pte C. Morriam. Salvage work carried out. Bathing in afternoon.	
10.		Demonstration of Platoon training by representative from G.H.Q. Very heavy rain continued. Companies at range. B.3.4.5.6. Battalion on Brigade duty. Platoon training in the afternoon.	08.5.G. 08.5.G.F.
11.		Platoon training, and range practice. field Hq Forbes returned from MATRINGHEM Conc. Draft of 65 ORs.	08.5.G.F.
12.} 13.}			
14.	1800	The Brigade addressed by the Corps Commander, Sir Charles Fergusson Bt, who expressed his thanks for work done, and successes achieved by the Brigade during the recent operations. The following N.C.O. awarded the Military Medal for gallant conduct during recent operations — L/Cpl W. Giffin G.	08.5.G.
15	11 am 2 pm	Church Parade - Rev J. Spence C.F. Brigadier parade for presentation of medal ribbons by the Divisional Commander	

Army Form C. 2118.

WAR DIARY
or
INTELLIGENCE SUMMARY.
(Erase heading not required.)

Map Reference 57° N.W. & N.E.

Place	Date	Hour	Summary of Events and Information	Remarks and references to Appendices
B.2.d.2.7.	Sept 15th		Operation Order No. issued. (Relief of 2/6 King's Liverpool Regt.). Major W. Mather assumed command of the Battn. owing to the absence of Lt Col J.G.P. Romans on leave in France. Major J.A. Smith, Cameronians and M.G. Corps, attached to the Battn.	Appendix VII. A/Sept.
	16th	9 a.m.	Battn. paraded and moved off via St LEGER, CROISILLES and BULLECOURT. A halt was made E. BULLECOURT for the midday meal. Battn. then proceeded to relieve "A" Bn of Support Bde. INCHY Sector. Relief complete at 9.45 p.m. Dispositions as follows:- Bn H.Q. D.5.c. 80.25. "B" & "C" Coys in D.5.c., HINDENBURG Support. "A" & "D" Coys (attached to Support Bn of Line Bde - 7th H.L.I.), in BUISSY SWITCH D.6.b.c.d. Relief was carried out without casualties but a considerable amount of gas was experienced.	A/Sept.
	17th		The morning passed quietly. About 10.30 a.m. a weak hostile attack on 155 Bde front was unsuccessful. (MOEUVRES Sector)	
		6.30 p.m.	Enemy brought down a heavy barrage on MOEUVRES Sector. S.O.S. was put up repeatedly. B.C. coys ordered to "Stand to". But an obscure throughout the night. Enemy had attacked strongly, and succeeded in breaking BF in MOEUVRES. 2nd R. Guards Division identified.	A/Sept.

WAR DIARY or INTELLIGENCE SUMMARY

Army Form C. 2118.

Place	Date	Hour	Summary of Events and Information	Remarks and references to Appendices
Saltwoodre	18		Orders received that Batt. would relieve 1/5 H.L.I. on night of 30/31st (see Batn. Order).	
	19	10 am	Orders for relief of H.L.I. cancelled and instructions issued that Bn. would be relieved by Bn. of 7th CANADIAN Inf.	
		1 pm	755 Pte. Pratt MOEYRES. During the enemy artillery shoot Several C.T. W.B. 10 & 20 were severely "D" d" at 120 & 126. Pte. CANADIANS by 11:30 pm. Pratt was taken by 124 & 126 to Pro. D.W.a. Bn. was removed to this D.W.a. Relieving 4th K.O.S.B. area (Coiffuel Sector).	
	20		Prisoners of C.Os at Bn. H.q.	
		9:20 pm	153 Bde on right of 10th Bn. would relieve 4th K.O.S.B. area (Coiffuel Sector). Relief commenced Bn. moved out from S/L "A" Coy 18th S.M. over House Lane (19a) to Hobart St. B & S.3 "D" Coy 40 B.H.R.T. St. 13.a 5.3 6 13.a 0.5. B.4.P. Coys. in immediate support to L.H. & R.H. of 1st Royal Scots.	

WAR DIARY
or
INTELLIGENCE SUMMARY

Army Form C. 2118.

A8

Place	Date	Hour	Summary of Events and Information	Remarks and references to Appendices
Moeuvres	Sept 1917		B. Coy. Posts 1. McDonald at B. Coy. at 13a.O.E. to 13d.9.2. C. Coy. at 19a.8.9. to 19.d.9.4.	B.
		3.30	Heavy enemy barrage on MOEUVRES.	
		Noon 3.45	Enemy attacked MOEUVRES strongly. 4th R.S. temporarily driven back but forward posts were retaken by immediate counter attack.	

Ref. Reference. 57½. N.E.

Army Form C. 2118.

WAR DIARY
or
INTELLIGENCE SUMMARY.
(Erase heading not required.)

Place	Date	Hour	Summary of Events and Information	Remarks and references to Appendices
MOEUVRES.	Sept. 22nd		Morning quiet. 156th Brigade line firmly established in front of MOEUVRES. "C" Coy. have established a block in our forward trench at E.30.d.2.7.	AQ.
			Orders received for extension of our boundary to D.22.a.0.7. D.30.d.0.3. K.3.a.0.8. by H.L.I. to take over line between old & new boundary.	
		8.45pm	Small enemy attack on left of Brigade front repelled. S.O.S. signals put up on our front guns by artillery. No attack on Brigade front.	
	23rd	10pm.	Batty trench at D.18.d.2.7 heavily shelled causing some casualties to Lewestock.	
			Morning quiet except for shelling at E.20.d.2.7. causing a few casualties to "C" Coy.	
			G.R.O. 19 of Sept. Third Army (Military Cross awarded to Capt B.C. Nelson & Capt. J.L. Smith.)	Lt. Col.

WAR DIARY or INTELLIGENCE SUMMARY

Army Form C. 2118.

War Diary 5/KNF

A 10

Place	Date	Hour	Summary of Events and Information	Remarks and references to Appendices
D/A 85	23rd		Third Army G.R.O. 19/15 Lieut. Distinguishes Conduct Medal awarded to C.S.M. Crowe A.L. & Sgt Smith W.L. Orders received that the Batt will be relieved and proceed to area D/y central. "A" "D" & 2 Platoons of "B" Coy relieved by 15th R.S.F. "C" Coy relieved by 4th K.O.S.B. 2 Platoons of "B" Coy relieved by 4th R.S.F. Night was quiet across the scene. Batt HQrs at D/A 85.	G
	24th 7:30 am		Battn move completed. "D" Coy in Left Support, "A" Coy in Support. "B" Coy's Lewis gun taken over by 1st A.R.S. as Batt hqr. "B" Coy's Lewis guns occupied by 251 Bgd. 2/51 Bgde. Brigade were informed of this and issued light issued an order for the R.F.A. to vacate the dugouts required.	B

Army Form C. 2118.

WAR DIARY
or
INTELLIGENCE SUMMARY.
(Erase heading not required.)

A.H.

Instructions regarding War Diaries and Intelligence Summaries are contained in F. S. Regs., Part II. and the Staff Manual respectively. Title pages will be prepared in manuscript.

Place	Date	Hour	Summary of Events and Information	Remarks and references to Appendices
O.14.a.85.	24	6.15 am	September. enemy put S.O.S. signal.	G.R.

Map Ref. 57cNE.

Army Form C. 2118.

WAR DIARY
or
INTELLIGENCE SUMMARY.
(Erase heading not required.)

a12

Place	Date	Hour	Summary of Events and Information	Remarks and references to Appendices
Rolincourt	Sept 24 contd.		The remainder of the day was quiet. Capt. A.D. Smith reported for duty from infantry course. 2/Lt. Michell James ,, ,, ,, from transport lines. Sgt. Baird & 2/Lt. Smith & Sgt. Gordon to U.K. to attend cadet school. Vide Army G.R.O. 19 Sept 21st. 9/Lt L.D. Watson awarded the Military Cross.	CR
	25th	6.15 am	S.O.S. signal put up by Bosche in front of MOEUVRES. Little attention noticed by 153 Brigade. Commanding officer back from Paris leave and took over command of the Battn. from Major Mathews. Orders received to move to area E.19 b & d cancelled owing to bad state of trenches.	CR

Army Form C. 2118.

WAR DIARY or INTELLIGENCE SUMMARY.
(Erase heading not required.)

A13

Place	Date	Hour	Summary of Events and Information	Remarks and references to Appendices
L.3.c.6.5.	Feb 27th	Particulars	At a Bn conference held at 1400 on 26th instructions were given to the Bn with them the following orders were issued. The Bn with the 4th Bedford Regiment were to cross the CANAL DU NORD and enter LEOPARD TRENCH immediately in rear of the 4th Royal Fus. and to there reorganise down the trench and down P19. A.V. All touch was gained with the GUARDS. DIV. ("A" Coy (Lt F L Huw) and "B" Coy (Lt H.P. Iideo.) were to form up in LEOPARD TRENCH and the CANAL and on the orders of the 63rd DIV. at ZERO+119. were to conform. Moving Plator by Plator on the 63rd DIV. but cut the head of LEOPARD TRENCH. These two Coys were to advance and no more each of two Platoon in extended order at LEOPARD TRENCH they were to take their dir.	App IV

Army Form C. 2118.

WAR DIARY
or
INTELLIGENCE SUMMARY.
(Erase heading not required.)

Instructions regarding War Diaries and Intelligence Summaries are contained in F. S. Regs., Part II. and the Staff Manual respectively. Title pages will be prepared in manuscript.

Place	Date	Hour	Summary of Events and Information	Remarks and references to Appendices
L.26.66.	24		They advanced and carry through to KANGAROO TRENCH. It meanwhile was met at E.27.d.4.9. "C" Coy (Capt B. Mirse B.S.) Coming in slow support) was to form garrison, and close with the having "A" Coy for the moved to KANGAROO. On arrival at KANGAROO "A" Coy was to feel out and consolidate where their left flank "B" Coy were to continue along the line of S.O.W. AV. till touch was gained with the GUARDS at CAT TRENCH. If however resistance was encountered "A" Coy was to some forward as to tribat. "C" Coy along A's place if "A" Coy was not able to do so. "C" Coy were to advance with "A" Coy were to either R.L. to advance along S.O.W. AV. by the line PIG. AV. touch with the GUARDS. Bat. "B" Coy were to consolidate that end of S.O.W. AV. and any that had been called up.	

Army Form C. 2118.

WAR DIARY
or
INTELLIGENCE SUMMARY.
(Erase heading not required.)

Place	Date	Hour	Summary of Events and Information	Remarks and references to Appendices
L29.c.6.b.	26th Sept		(continued) that they were to reconnoitre the ground between SOW. AV. and KANGAROO. K. "C" Coy. closed sectors in support and in ZEBRA. D. Company sent to reconnoitre country and ascertain the ground between KANGAROO and SOW. AV. Otherwise the men were to rest and sleep as much as possible in ZEBRA. Each of the other 3 Companies were ordered to inform D"Coy accordingly. The allocation of Company frontages was left to the Officers Commanding Companies on the spot. As soon as trenches had been occupied each Company was to send 1 Platoon to form a support line on the high ground between Sous Terrene & the Hindenburg Support from Kangaroo to bat. (The above scheme will hereafter be referred to as the Normal Scheme.) The Battalion assembly points for their operations was given in Brigade Orders as the area between the two main trenches of the Hindenburg line at E.19.B.4. The forward trench being out of the area. Battalion Headquarters at E.19.d.7.6. Originally this area was to had been occupied by 0200 on 26th Sept. but a representation being made that the area was under view from BOURLON the move was postponed 24 hours & the Battalion arrived at area of assembly by 0200 on 27th Sept. From here Companies were ordered to move to relieve the band du Nord by the Northern Trench of Hindenburg line by hero +60 where they were to deploy behind the 4th R.S. who at that time should be in Leopard Trench.	

Map Ref 5⁹ C.N.E.

Army Form C. 2118.

WAR DIARY
or
INTELLIGENCE SUMMARY.
(Erase heading not required.)

O.16

Place	Date	Hour	Summary of Events and Information	Remarks and references to Appendices
L3c6l.	Sept. 27	Zero.	A runner post was to be established on the Canal at Zero +60. On no account was the Battalion to become involved in the operation of the 4th R.S. until these had reached Leopard Avenue. Zero hour was at 0520 + at that time our guns put down a heavy barrage to which the enemy replied with increasing vigour. At 0605 "A" + "B" Coys began to advance up towards the Canal did not was the Northern trench of the Hindenburg Line. "D" Coy had already moved off close behind the 4th R.S. Owing to the enemy barrage (including T.Ms) to the line + to M.Gd fire the 4th R.S. were soon held up + incurred many casualties. The Battalion of the Bedfordshire Regt. of the 63rd Division on our left were also held up. This occurred on the 4th R.S. reaching Lord Street. Ammunition + bombs ran short. 2/Lt. Brooks who had been sent forward with Pte. Hutcheson to report progress were able to assist 4th R.S. (who had suffered severely by enemy M.G. T.M. + gun fire) to reorganise. 2/Lt. Brooks also obtained the assistance of Capt. W. Rodger of 13. Coy. M.G. Coy. who brought his gun right forward + though wounded continued to render valuable assistance. Meantime no great progress had been made though the 4th R.S. suffered severely + at about 0900 Capt. S. Smith determined to press forward with his company. He came to this determination on his own initiative though as a matter of fact the Adjutant was on his way out to move the Battalion forward. Capt. Smith advanced two platoons rushed the enemy on the west bank of the Canal + crossed it with his other platoons in close conflict, driving the enemy posts on the east bank back to Leopard Trench. Here while organising his Company for the second phase this gallant officer was killed by fire from the widetern bank. His determined action gained the passage of the Canal for our troops. The Adjutant had by this time arrived at the firing line was able to report	

Army Form C. 2118.

WAR DIARY
or
INTELLIGENCE SUMMARY.
(Erase heading not required)

Mahhk. 5/C.M.E.

Place	Date	Hour	Summary of Events and Information	Remarks and references to Appendices
L3c6.6.	5/11.			X17
	3/		by 1000 that the Battalion was started on the second phase of the operations. C. Company undertook the operation originally allotted D. Coy. as that Company had been reduced to one officer.	
			On reaching Lion Trench 150-200 Germans surrendered to A. Coy. Here a halt was made as one of the 63rd Division appeared to be on our left. These arrived about quarter of an hour later.	
			Owing to heavy M.G. fire on our left front A. & B. Coys. were definitely held up on the line Lion - Jackal Rig Avenue in which had stands C. Coy. had effected a junction with the Guards Brigade capturing about 200 prisoners.	
			Bombing was then resorted to & B. Coys. advanced of Lion Trench where touch was gained with the Guards about 1230. At large pockets of Germans still held the northern extremity of Kangaroo "A" Coys. were however able to occupy all but the northern extremity until the addition of the 63rd Division about 1430 put the whole trench in our hands. Consolidation along the line originally detailed was proceeded with by A. O. & D. Coys. C. Coy. held a fragment line along the ridge to the immediate front.	

Casualties.

	Officers.	Other Ranks.
Killed.	3.	8.
Wounded.	1.	29.
Missing.	-	11

Prisoners of War Captured.
474.

Booty:
Trench Mortars 3.
Machine Guns.   36.
Rifles.   170.
Anti Tank Rifle. 1

Also a considerable quantity of other booty.

WAR DIARY
or
INTELLIGENCE SUMMARY.

Army Form C. 2118.

Place	Date	Hour	Summary of Events and Information	Remarks and references to Appendices
L3.c.	Feb. 28		Bn. in trenches. Col'nel Holiday A.D. Coy in KANGAROO. "B" in SOW TRENCH Bn. HQ at E.29d.4.6. (ZEBRA TR.) Lt Col Clement D.S.O. takes over command of Bn with Lt Col Legat D.S.O. so on leave. Major Walker takes command of Bn. Bath visiting. Bombs rifle exploders. Lewis gun. Boys on parade in K.3. 2 N.4. cabbage nuclus. 2 N.45 sight & range.	
	29		Lent return showed expected in cabbage nuclus morning. 12 noon. Nuclus moved from trenches lines under Lt M.H.I. Gutcomb M.C. Capt Mackern retired from trenches to B.C. and takes over Hooton as adjutant. Lt Billou assumes duties of adjutant. Lt M. Henshaw M.C. and takes over No. "D" Coy. suc Capt. J.L. Smith killed.	

19

Army Form C. 2118.

WAR DIARY
or
INTELLIGENCE SUMMARY.
(Erase heading not required.)

A.17

Place	Date	Hour	Summary of Events and Information	Remarks and references to Appendices
L.3.C.61.	Sept. 29	2 p.m.	Lt. McNish reports to C.O. for duty and posted to "D" Coy. Draft of 29 O.R. arrives. Capt. Ross arrived from leave to U.K. and assumes command of "A" Coy vice Lt. Ross to Lucknow. Battalion on fatigue as same area as yesterday. Instructions received for Bn. to be ready to move after 9 am 1st Oct.	
	30			

J Ronan Lt Col
6/7th R. Cameron[?]

Strength in the field 31st August 1914   O 626
                                          OR 626
to 2nd Sept 1914   Sgts 98
                                          ___
                                          126

Officers

Increases
Lt Carthallin
Imperial Lutton
Lt F Chipster
2nd Lt R Turner
Capt Farmerstown
Support Lees
Capt Matchew
L Arkous   Hon Surgeon
Lt Johnston
Lt McNaughton
Mr T.C. Ward   Hon Surgeon
Maj G. Murphy   Hon Surgeon
Lt C. Pinton   "
Capt Ashworth
2nd Lt Thomson   Hon Apoplactic
Lt Aspen   Ferrise
Pte G. Smith
Pte Mansfield
2nd Lt M. Wilson
Pte A. Morrall
Lieut Macsurence

Decreases
Sergeant Wilson   killed
Sergt Balmont
Mr G. Hutton   "
Mr McGentlish   "
2nd Lt Loures   wounded
Lt F. Chipster   died of wound
Lt R. Turner
Capt Stephen
Capt Larston   "
Mr McCrawson
Mr Warmburgen
Mackintosh   "
Mr Kept
Mr Morris   "
Mr Morrison   to hero
Mr McChyppen
Mr Scfulson
Lt Carlmanne   to hopee
Lt Brewton
Sgt Bray
Lt Rice   "
Mr Mathous   to hospee
Sgt Johnson
Sgt a Dunlop

Increases	
Reinforcements	0
from Rouen	6
" "	3
Hospital	1
Leave	6
" "	2
Hospital	1
Drivers	1
Other Causes	1
Total	20

Decreases	
Killed	4
Wounded	6
Wounded (gas)	112
To Hospital	2
Leave	4
Last	3
Drivers	1
Drivers	2
Lost (sick)	
Other Causes	
Total	24

	0
	98
	18
	48
	46
	16
	38
	253

	30
	119
	25
	897
	26
	112
	31
	35
	5
	467

War Diary
of
1/1st Carnarvons (SR)
1st to 31st October 1918

War Diary 51° N.E.

Army Form C. 2118.

WAR DIARY
or
INTELLIGENCE SUMMARY.
(Erase heading not required.)

Place	Date	Hour	Summary of Events and Information	Remarks and references to Appendices
L.3.c.	Oct 1		Instructions received for Bn. to move to Div. HQ. area at L.3.a.	
			Bn. marched.	
			Capt. W.C. Maclean M.C. to hospital.	
		3½	Commanding Officer attended Brigade conference and orders received to be ready to move at ½ hrs notice.	R.H.
			attacking at 180.	
	2nd	180	153 Bde attacked but situation obscure.	
		1900	Battn. in Div. orders area. 153ʳᵈ attack Battn. HQ at L.3.c.6.6.	
			Bn. in reserve area.	
			Brig. Gen. Riggs wounded from here to W.K. died from wounds.	Q. H.
			Lt. Col. Rameau D.S.O. to command 61 Bde.	
			nucleus.	
	3rd		Bn. in advance in reserve area.	R.J.
		11.30	Instructions received for Bn. commanders to remain in area.	
			C.O. attend Bde. conference.	B.J.

WAR DIARY
or
INTELLIGENCE SUMMARY.
(Erase heading not required.)

Army Form C. 2118.

Mch Rch 57° NE   a 2

Place	Date	Hour	Summary of Events and Information	Remarks and references to Appendices
L.3.c.	Oct 4 1918			
		Mid. N. O.	carried out patrols at G.81.	(A)
			Coy commanders reconnoitred own area.	
			Unofficial report that enemy had surrendered.	
		1pm	Hostile aircraft located Bn area.	
			Instructions received for Capt. H.C. McLEOD to proceed to W.K. on six months duty.	
		5pm	Capt. H.C. Maclean M.C. to W.K.	
		6.30	Instructions received for Bn to move to area T. 2. 3. 4.	(B)
		9pm	Bn paraded and marched off.	
		11.30	Bn in new area T. 3. c. and half for the day.	
			2/Lt. Morison reported for duty and posted to B Coy.	
			Lt. W. Rennie D.L.O. resumes command.	
			Major Maclean on advance party.	

Army Form C. 2118.

WAR DIARY
or
INTELLIGENCE SUMMARY.

Map O.A 51° N.E.

LENS II. 1/100,000.

Place	Date	Hour	Summary of Events and Information	Remarks and references to Appendices
Acheux	Oct. 6.		Instructions received for Bn. to march to VAUX VRAUCOURT. leaving starting point J.3.c.5.5. at 0940.	
	7th	09.30	Bn. paraded & moved off.	
		13.00	Bn. arrived at VAUX VRAUCOURT for TINCQUETTE.	
		18.30	Bn. arrived at TINCQUETTE and moved to billets at PENIN.	
Penin	8th		Bn. in billets at PENIN. Coys reorganising and cleaning up.	
	9th	08.30	Commanding Officer at conference at Divisional Hq.	
		19.00	C.O. held conference with Coy commanders. Bn. as open for reinforcements.	
	10th		Leave for Commanding Officer at CAIL arranging & Battalion reorganising and re-equipping	

Wah. Ref. 52. Horo

Army Form C. 2118.

WAR DIARY
or
INTELLIGENCE SUMMARY.
(Erase heading not required.)

Place	Date	Hour	Summary of Events and Information	Remarks and references to Appendices
JENIN.	October 11.		Coys in training in vicinity of Litilto from 0830 to 1230.	
	12.		Without instruction of Coy.	
	13.		Coys in training from 0830 to 1230.	
	14.		Bn. Church Parade.	
			Coys in training at I.19.	
			Letter from Lieut. Gen. J.H.G. BYNG. K.C.B. K.C.M.G. M.V.O. expressing thanks for services rendered by Div. in recent operations.	
	15.		Coys in training in training area.	
	16.		Coys in training near Litilto. (Night operations from 1900 to 2200.)	
	17.		Coys in training. The MILITARY MEDAL awarded to the following: 365393. 2/Sgr. GALBRAITH. 266045. Pte HUTCHIESON. 33854. Pte. TRAINER. 266049. Pte HAZLETT.	
	18.		Coys in training near Litilto. Message received from Bde that Bn was ordered to move tomorrow. Night operation cancelled.	

Army Form C. 2118.

WAR DIARY
or
INTELLIGENCE SUMMARY.
(Erase heading not required.)

Place	Date	Hour	Summary of Events and Information	Remarks and references to Appendices
Brins	Oct. 19.		Instructions received from Bgde that Bns will move east to CHATEAU DE LA HAIE. Mgralion order 60.	Appd. I.
	20.	0730	Bn. moved and moved off.	B.
		Noon	Bn. arrives CHATEAU DE LA HAIE.	
		0900	Bn. marched and reached to BULLY-MONTIGNY. Col Romeril took over 151 Bn. Major Wallis assumed command of Bn.	
	21.	0/000	Bn. marched out and reached AUBY.	
	22.		Bn. in training at AUBY.	
	23.		Bn. in training at AUBY. Bn SBR's inspected by Bde Gas Off.	
	24.	0930	Btn moved and reached to COUTICHES.	
	25.	0900	Bn reporting roads between COUTICHES and FLINES.	
	26.	0900	Bn repairing roads between COUTICHES and FLINES. Major Wallis granted four days leave to U.K. Capt D R Vincent in command actg of Bn.	

Army Form C. 2118.

WAR DIARY
or
INTELLIGENCE SUMMARY.
(Erase heading not required.)

Mob. Ref. Ret. 44 Victoria.

A.6

Instructions regarding War Diaries and Intelligence Summaries are contained in F. S. Regs., Part II. and the Staff Manual respectively. Title pages will be prepared in manuscript.

Place	Date 1918	Hour	Summary of Events and Information	Remarks and references to Appendices
LECELLES	27.	0800	Bn. paraded and marched to LECELLES. H.Q. attends conference at Bde. Hq. Instructions received that Bn. will take over the line. Bn. moves take over outposts from 9th Royal SUSSEX.	G.H.
	28.	1100	Bn. paraded and marched to Mont Du Roy where guides of 9th Royal SUSSEX were met. Dispositions as follows. Bn. Hq. T.29d.4.4. A. Coy. T.28.c.8.0. B Coy. T.29.c.8.9. C Coy. T.36.a.s.4. D Coy. T.28.c.2.8. Transport and Gn. Store T.34.a.4.4.	G.H.
	29.		Bn. carrying out tours in Tactical Cy Hours for posts at Bn. H.Q.	G.H.
	30.	1000	A Coy elated with Gas. No casualties. Inhabitants were killed. 9 horses wounded and 3 killed. Bn's carried out Tactical Scheme. Remainder of Bn. patrols	G.H.
	.	2300	Patrol went out was followed the enemy wire	G.H.

Army Form C. 2118.

WAR DIARY
or
INTELLIGENCE SUMMARY.
(Erase heading not required.)

Place	Date	Hour	Summary of Events and Information	Remarks and references to Appendices
MoAT Dv Proj.	Oct 1918 30. 31.		October 1918 — Army withdrawing on Bde front. Otro, the men counted and normal condition resumed.	

Strength in the field 30th September 1918.   O   OR
                      to 31st October 1918.   24   #95
                                               20   #35
                      Decrease # Decrease 63

Increase

	O	OR
Reinforcement	0	—
From Hospital	3	10
Detachment T	1	60
Other Causes	—	—
	3	108
	7	173

Decrease

	O	OR
To Hospital	1	36
Killed	—	—
Wounded	—	4
Missing	—	—
Lourdes	3	14
Leave	4	163
Other causes	3	19
	11	236

Officers

Increase

Major Smith 1st Joint
Lieut Nattrass 1st "
  "   Kerr
  "   Lollard 3 "
  "   Morrison 1/c pmt
Hieut Bowen "   "
   "   West 1st Hospital

Decrease

Lt Col Holmes 1/1 "
Major Whatton
left return UK
Lieut Kerr
  "   Willis Col 2
  "   Kerr
Capt Glauworth 1/5
  "   Hiatt Cosite
  "   Anderson Col 1
  "   Goldicutt
  "   Stratton pln to UK

Army Form C. 2118.

WAR DIARY
or
INTELLIGENCE SUMMARY.
(Erase heading not required.)

War Diary
of
4th Bn. the Cameronians (Scottish Rifles)

November 1918

Volume XLII

War Diary / Intelligence Summary — Army Form C. 2118

Place	Date	Hour	Summary of Events and Information	Remarks and references to Appendices
Mont. Dn. Roy.	November 1917		Instructions received that Bn. will take over the line from	APPEX. I.
	1		4th Royal Scots. Quartermaster Rd. & Relief complete 1900.	
			Bn. Hq. at T.29c.8.7. "A" Coy. T.24.a.3.4. "B" Coy. T.18.c.2.7.	
MAISNIL DE NIVELLE			"C" Coy. K.25a.8.2. "D" Coy. K.30.E.1.4.	
		0100	Patrols under 2/Lt Chundal & 2/Lt Heath, found enemy posts up to enemy line.	
		0335	Patrol under 2/Lt Watson D.G. proceeded to bridge at Rabais T. When they were met by enemy M.G. fire. 2/Lt Watson and 2/Lt Walker advanced & ran crossing bridge but were held up.	
			20 O.R.s on other side. Big 11 gas shells near Hq. 10 minute long fires.	
			The remainder of Day was quiet.	
	2	7 a.m.	Enemy opened up for a few minutes of Lewis operator over Hq.	APPEX. 2.
		11 a.m.	Relief complete. Coys in the new quarters. A Coy Hq at	
			K.32.b.15. Hq Coy K.32.a.4.6. B Coy T.32 a.4.7.	

Army Form C. 2118.

WAR DIARY
or
INTELLIGENCE SUMMARY.
(Erase heading not required.)

Place	Date	Hour	Summary of Events and Information	Remarks and references to Appendices
MARIE DE NEVILLE	Nov 3.	1100	"B" Coy Dy Church parade. H.E. aimed shot K.B. on 1 hour. No casualties.	
		1500	"A" Coy went to scan Pits. Others Coys inspection of kit. Pits Note sent by M. to K31c23.	G. 2/1
	Mon.		Shoot was fairly light with 3 mg active. Several rounds of "B" by 7.T.M. She... had B.W. bursting over R.K. coming from the Coton window.	
	4			
		A.M.	Enemy shelled army R.3c & 2.4. 50 rounds H.E.	
		1130	6 enemy battalions brought down by our planes.	
		12.30	One enemy balloon brought down no fires.	
			Remainder of day was very quiet.	
	5.	1100	Commanding officer attack B.de Retirees at B.de Dy.	mH
		1100	The method of warfare being discussed.	APPENDIX II
			"A" Coy relieved "D" Coy in the line.	

Mil. Ref. Sht. HI 15000.   A3   Army Form C. 2118.

WAR DIARY
or
INTELLIGENCE SUMMARY.
(Erase heading not required.)

Place	Date	Hour	Summary of Events and Information	Remarks and references to Appendices
Marie du Rivage	Nov 6	1030	Commanding Officer held conference of Coy Commanders at Bn Coy HQ.	APPENDIX IV
		2200	Fighting Patrol from K26a47 met with MG fire and returns from river at 2245.	A/C
	7	0400	Patrol to K26a47 met with MG fire and returned to own lines at 0430.	
			Flooding increased very much during the day - inundation extending from POINT de la VERNETTE to K20c38.	A/C
	8	0600	Left outpost company (B) reported that the enemy had withdrawn from JARD CANAL. This company at once began to move forward from rafts from LE LONG BUHOT & RIVER ESCAUT at K26a47 and thereafter crossed the river, the inundation, and finally the JARD CANAL.	
		0615	C Company reported to OC Section 412 Coy RE to carry rafts and RE material from MARIE de NIVELLE	
		0945	D Company was concentrated in LE LONG SPURT ready to carry on in support of outposts forming the bridgehead	A/C

WAR DIARY
or
INTELLIGENCE SUMMARY

Army Form C. 2118.

Place	Date	Hour	Summary of Events and Information	Remarks and references to Appendices
MARIE de NIVELLE	Nov 8	0930	The whole of the Brigade Company (B) were the JARD CANAL and further on RIVER ESCAUT completed at 1030. HERGNIES reported clear of the enemy.	
		1100	Brigadier Genl. and [Staff] reports on a position reported to them are [placed] to the later details to reconnoitre and clear the ground in K29. 1300. [Supp]	
			in K29 reported clear of the enemy.	
		1215	Cyclists moved through [village]. 1500 Remainder of battalion (Hd.qtrs. and 2 Coys.) moved forward to (6 long) BUTOT. C Coy to HERGNIES. On arrival of [advance] at 6.30 pm they had of the Battalion are two men seen.	
			Bridge at COUPURE, (K.27 of 41)	
		1800	Battalion less two platoons of B.Coy on left flank & 7 Royal Scots in other hand, billeted in K.21.D.	tc
HERGNIES	9	0830	The Brigade continues its march east through MONT d PERUWELZ and BONSECOURS to BLATON, Cameronians forming 7th Bde advanced guard.	APPENDIX V
			[Rest] of the march [quiet]	
		1500	The [battn] less two platoons on left flank of 45 Royal Scots were	
BLATON			billeted for the night in BLATON.	10

WAR DIARY or INTELLIGENCE SUMMARY

Army Form C. 2118.

Place	Date	Hour	Summary of Events and Information	Remarks and references to Appendices
BLATON	11/11	0830	156th Inf Bde Order No 70 received 0200 & the Brigade continued its advance eastwards. The Battalion formed part of the main body and followed Bde Hqrs. passed the starting point at 0635. 4th Royal Scots were advance guard to the Brigade. SIRAULT was reached without incident. At this place radio orders were received from Brigade to push through 4th R.S. and cover the advance of the Brigade – Final objective – a line east of ERBAUT, to cover that village. The advanced guard consisted of 7th Scottish Rifles C Coy 52nd Bn. M.G.C. 1 Battery 95th Bde. R.F.A. 1 Platoon Corps Cyclists	MAPS/10/17 VI
SIRAULT	1300		all under command of OC 7th Scottish Rifles. The advanced guard were about to be ready to move at 1300 but did not move then. VIII Corps Cyclists reported hostile MG fire from the direction of VACROSSE and HERCHIES. Owing to this information when there arrived to A Coy to deploy on the Brigade front and advance on HERCHIES. B Coy with one section M.Gs were sent to watch along the northern flank as that flank was reported on account of 52nd Division final objective for the day being NEUFMAISON – Eloy etc	

Army Form C. 2118.

Maps: Sheet 45 Ypres

WAR DIARY
or
INTELLIGENCE SUMMARY.
(Erase heading not required.)

Place	Date	Hour	Summary of Events and Information	Remarks and references to Appendices
SIRAULT	NOV 10	1400	Cmdts reptd + D Coy on left deployed about 1500 yds in rear of 'A' Coy and advanced in support of that Coy. - Batt HQrs - House in battery astride of SIRAULT - C Coy 52R. M.G. + Battn RTR + Cyclist platn remains with Battn Hqrs. 157 Rgle advancing on the South through BOIS au BAUDOUR mounts to direct a fire to front north and thence HERCHIES. VACROSSE. No touch was obtained with them. Reported touch with Ist Corps at NEUFMAISON and none East of that astride. The advance continued about 1420 B Coy moving first then A Coy, C 26 & 28. the direction of HERCHIES as VACRESSE was met with no fire from then bought forward Pon Atym, then shelled at farm C 26 & 28 came into action and one of great assistance in overcoming opposition Remnants of Battery to SIRAULT held with come into action. Good progress was made and by 1630 we had entered and passed through HERCHIES. Enthusiastic reception by the inhabitants. Am Hqrs.	
HERCHIES		1700	established = HERCHIES. C+D Coys drew withdrawn into bivouac Owing to the difficulty of invading adv. country and contact in the dark. And B Coys entrenched the action as they were heav at about Bonjean from ERBAUT by 1700. MG fire HERCHIES at that time. Much expensively attention from Bosch artillery.	

Map Ypres Sheet 7 1:40,000   A7   Army Form C. 2118.

WAR DIARY
or
INTELLIGENCE SUMMARY.
(Erase heading not required.)

Place	Date	Hour	Summary of Events and Information	Remarks and references to Appendices
HERCULES	Nov 10	9:00	Two platoons of D Coy were put at disposal of O.C. A Coy in order to enable him to push on to his objective. In spite of the movement, above said still delayed and C Coy was instructed to more flanking movement always in conjunction with other two Coys. This moved in D 20 b and a as objective. This move commenced at 20.15. Every man at first also had at about midnight the enemy's resistance was beaten, he retired and by 0100 on 11th all Coys had reached their final objective and were up a line approximately D8 central, D8 central to D 21 central. 2 MGs and 17 prisoners were captured in this operation. Our casualties, 3 killed, 1 died of wounds, 7 wounded & missing. All companies dug themselves in. During OC B Coy did usefully good work in consolidating line Coy and reached his final objective with no complete (except casualties), a noticeable difference in temperament improving its audibility the different actions of the enemy and the fact that no prisoners were more hostile.	

Map Alfa Sheet 45
1:40,000

WAR DIARY
or
INTELLIGENCE SUMMARY.
(Erase heading not required.)

Army Form C. 2118.

Place	Date	Hour	Summary of Events and Information	Remarks and references to Appendices
ERBAUT	Nov 11	0930	15S Bn Pde. March through outpost line held by the Bn. Pde. to our coys	
			was withdrawn and Battalion in ERBAUT	
		1030	Were relieved from Brigade that hostilities would cease at 1100	
		1430	Battalion moved to HERCHIES and billeted there	B/Co. Lt. Col. P. Ramsey DSO ftc
HERCHIES	12		Rest day.	Appointed Temp. Comdg. 157 Inf. Bde. ftc
	13		Cleaning equipment and clothing. Conference of coy. officers regarding	ftc
			sanitation of the Battalion	
	14		Cleaning parades.	ftc
	15	0700	Party from the Battalion left for MONS to take part in the official entry	ftc
			of G.O.C. 1st Army into the town. Lt. Ramsey in command of the	
			Battalion Party. Returned at 1930.	
	16	1000	Inspection of Battalion by Brig. Gen. Baggett.	ftc
		1030	Battalion fell out in marching order & prepared so as to produce surprise in case	ftc
			coy.	
	17	1100	A coy. attended Divisional Thanksgiving Service at HERCHIES	ftc
		1430	Brigade Thanksgiving Service at METRONIES	ftc

Army Form C. 2118.

WAR DIARY
or
INTELLIGENCE SUMMARY.
(Erase heading not required.)

Place	Date	Hour	Summary of Events and Information	Remarks and references to Appendices
HERCHIES	18	0900	Training parades 0900 - 1200. Monday programme commenced.	A/C
	19	1030	Inspection of the Battalion by the B.G.C. 156 Inf. Bde.	A/C
	20		Training parades 0900 - 1200	A/C
	21		do	A/C
	22		do	A/C
	23		do	A/C
	24	1030	Church Parade in HERCHIES	A/C
	25		Training parades 0900 - 1200. Educational training started. Introductory lectures at 1500. Classes commenced in Arithmetic, English, Bookkeeping, Shorthand, French, German, also instructional parades in Boxing.	
	26		Regual Fgt.trig & Lewis Gun & Military Training 0830 - 1130. Educational 1200 - 1300	A/C
LENS	27	1215	Battalion moves to LENS and 5 kilos north of HERCHIES billets there.	A/C Appendix VII & VIII
Nr Tournai 1/100 000	28		Cleaning up billets	A/C
	29		do	A/C
	30		St Andrew's Day. Observed as a holiday. Major R. BLAIR returned from UK. Lt Col T.G. P. BOWRES DSO took over Command	A/C

Army Form C. 2118.

WAR DIARY
INTELLIGENCE SUMMARY.
(Erase heading not required.)

Place	Date	Hour	Summary of Events and Information	Remarks and references to Appendices
LENS	Nov 30		Command of 1/6 Inf Bde. Major R Blair	
			3q C and move to UK.	
			took over Command of the Battalion	
			R Blair Major	

Strength in the field 31/7/78   O. 20   445
                      do 30/7/78   26   581
                          Increase   6   Increase 149

Increase

Reinforcements   5   34
From Hospital   2   66
Detachment & other   9   226
causes
                      ---   ---
                      16   329

Decrease

To Hospital   1   34
Killed   -   3
Wounded   -   16
Missing   -   3
Sources   3   4
Leave   5   107
Other causes   1   13
                      ---   ---
                      10   180

Officers

Increase

Lt Col. Romanis from 13y Bde
Lieut. Tillin P.O.
Officer Thomson N.S.   ? Leave
   "   Cullen S   "
   "   Abbott B.A   " Leave
   "   Anderson N.T   "
   "   Aitchison J.   " Hospital
Capt.   Aitken R.S   "
Capt.   Smith R.S.   " Brigade
Lieut. Bird N.S   "
Officer Lonsley W   "
   "   White Pn   " ?
   "   Harvey Y   " ?
Lieut   Leckie S   "
Major   Blair R   "
Lieut   Smith A.W.   "

Decrease

L. Dewar to To Canon
Ythanley, H.   "
L. Smith Cur   "
Mr N.S Thomson   To Canon
Mr S. Cullen   "
Mr W.T Anderson   "
Capt E. Phillips   "
Mr G. Brooke   "
Capt H. S. Smith   To Brigade
        Aitken R.S. "   Hospt

Operation Orders   I
by
Captain D.K. Nelson O/C Coy
1/7th Cameronians (Sco Rifles)
                        1st November 16

1. Battalion will relieve the 7th Royal Scots in the support line tonight.

2. Coys will take over as under:
   A Coy 7th SR from No 3 Coy. 7th R.S.
   B "   "   "   "   2   "   "
   C "   "   "   "   4   "   "
   D "   "   "   "   1   "   "
   The first three Coys are in the support line and the other in support.

3. D Coy will leave their present headqrs at 1500.
   A, B & C Coys will leave their present headqrs at 1700. Batt. H.Q. will leave at 1630.

4. Guides will report as under:
   A Coy at Bridge at T.29.B.5.3. at 1700.
   B & C Coys at Coy Headqrs at 1700.

5. Cookers will be handed over. C.Q.M.S of each Coy will report to OC Coy at 1600 to hand over. 1 N.C.O. per Coy will report to Coy HQ. 7th R.S. to take over cookers.

2

6. H.Q. & Sgts will remain at present Coy
Headqrs till arrival of ration limbers and
will then proceed to new Coy area.
7. Coy Storemen will report to QM at Transport
lines forthwith. They should have with them
strengths of Rations and Coy Headquarters.
8. Guides. The Intelligence Officer will arrange
for 1 scout per Coy to remain at present Coy
Headqrs and conduct limbers to new area.
9. S.O.S. Grenades. Green over Red over Green -
will be taken over by Coys.
10. 1 box Grenades will be sent from Transport
lines to A, B, & C Coys.
+ 12. O.C. "E" Coy will detail 1 Officer and 1 Section
to be ready at any time in the event of
unusual quietness to reconnoitre east of bridge
at K.26.A.4.7.
13. The Sigs Officer will arrange to take over
communications at 1600 and the Intelligence Officer
the Battalion O.P. at the same hour.
14. Officers Valises may be taken at the discretion
of O.C. Coy. Returning Ration Limbers will be used
to convey them to Transport lines if they desire.

3

not to take them.

15) On completion of relief Officers charges will be returned to the Transport lines.

16) In order to preserve continuity of patrols, 1st Royal Scots will leave sufficient personnel in the line on night of 1st/2nd Nov. to carry out the usual patrols.

Personnel from 7th Cameronians will accompany these patrols.

17) Completion of relief will be sent to Battn HQ by code word "AUSTRIA".

18) Mess Cart, Maltese Cart and Limbers will report to Battn HQ at 1530 to carry Kits &c to New Area.

Sgd. D. McWilliam
Lt. & Adjt.

Operation Orders by
Captain D R Nelson MC cmdg
1/7 Bn. Cameronians (Sc. Rif)

2 Nov. 18

1. The following adjustment of the line will be carried out tonight.

Letter "D" Company will relieve "C" Company 2nd Bn West Yorks in outpost line on road K 32 B 3.3 to K 33 D 1.1. A liaison post with 8th Division will be established in CHATEAU de FORET. OC "D" Coy will arrange his own guides.

A + B Coys 7 S.R. will be relieved in present outpost line by B + C Coys 4 Royal Scots respectively.

These companies will each send a guide to Bn. Hq at 16.15 to guide 4 RS companies to their areas.

Letter "C" Coy. will remain in its present position.

On completion of relief from present line "A" Company will relieve a Company of 2nd Bn West Yorks in support at FARM K 32 A 3.2 and "B" Company will take over billets vacated by "D" Coy I this battalion location HAUTE RIVE and BURIDON.

The necessary reconnaissances will be carried out forthwith.

Contd/

Teams for Cookers and Lewis Gun limbers of
A, B and D Coys will report to Bn HQ at 17.00

Store SOS signals in the case of A & B Coys
will be handed over, and in the case of
D Coy will be taken over.
No tools or grenades will be taken over or
handed over.

As soon as 'B' Coy has taken over position
in HAUTERIVE and BURIDON O.C. Coy will
inform O.C. Coy 7RS there. That Coy of 7RS
will then rejoin their battalion.

Ration limbers for D, A & B Coys will report
to Bn HQrs, that of C Coy will proceed
direct to its company area.

Bn HQrs remain at present position.

Relief complete will be notified to Bn HQ
by Code-word HELL.

2/11/18

D. McWilliam Lt. & Adjt
1/7 Cameronians

Operation order
by
Capt J.R. Nelson M.C. Comdg
5th Cameronians
(S.R.Rifles)
5th Nov 1916

"A" Coy will relieve "D" Coy and "B" Coy
will relieve "C" Coy in the Outpost
line tonight.
Relieving Coys will move at dusk
and will take over dispositions of the
Coys as at present.
Cookers will be handed over.
Rations will be sent to Battn. H.Q. from
which they will be forwarded to
new areas. Guides will be provided
by Battn. H.Q.
Valises will be sent to new areas by
returning ration limbers.
One Platoon of "C" Coy under an Officer
will remain with "B" Coy till 2359.
Completion of relief will be notified
to these H.Q. by code word "GAITERS"

D. McWilliams Lt & Adjt
5th Cameronians

Provisional Operation Orders
by
Captain J E Nelson MC Comdg
fifth Camerons (Sco. Rifles)
                                5th Novr. 1918

1. LEFT FRONT LINE Coy. As soon as the left front
   line Coy has ascertained that the enemy
   has withdrawn from TARD CANAL the
   Coy will move across River ESCAUT at K.26.A.4.7

2. RIGHT SUPPORT Coy. The Right Support Coy
   will be prepared to move in support to
   left front Coy

3. LEFT SUPPORT Coy. Left support Coy will at once
   report in skeleton order and without Lewis
   Guns to OC Section R.E. for carrying
   bridging material

4. RIGHT FRONT LINE Coy Right Front line Coy
   will stand fast.

5. Move. Before moving all Coys except
   left support Coy, as mentioned above, will
   assume fighting order and will make
   a Coy dump of greatcoats and haversacks
   at a suitable place rear Coy Headqrs.
   One cook per Coy will remain in charge
   of the dump and the cookers

-2-

6. Transport. A warning order will be issued to the Transport Officer on receipt of which he will detail a NCO with teams to proceed to Headqrs of each Coy to collect Cookers and rendezvous them near R.25.B.7.1. LE LONG BUHOT. They will join 1st line Transport as it passes.

Mess Cart, Maclean Cart, one tool limber will report to Battn Headqrs and will join 1st line Transport at Bridge T.29.C.8.5. The Transport Officer will collect these.

7. Dumps Orders regarding the collecting of Greatcoats and haversacks will be issued later.

8. Nucleus In the event of a move and until further orders Nucleus will remain with Transport lines.

(Sd) D. McWilliam
Lt/a/adjt
1/1th Cameronians
(Sco Rifles)

Operation Orders V
by
Captain D. D. Nilson, M.C. Commg
7/7th Cameronians (S.R.) Rifles
8-11-18

1. The Brigade will advance tomorrow 9-11-18 and secure the line of the ANTOING – PÉRUWELZ CANAL between F.21.D.5.2 and G.15.C.6.5.

2. Orders of March
   (a) Advance Guard - 7th Royal Scots
   (b) Bde. HQ
   (c) 4th Royal Scots
   (d) 7th Cameronians

3. The Battalion will passing starting point Cross Road at K.24.B.15.9.0 at 0730

4. Order of March. Bn. Hqrs A. C. D. B.

5. Lewis Gun Limbers will march in rear of Companies. Remainder of transport in rear of the Battalion.

6. A distance of 100 yards will be maintained between Companies.

7. March discipline. Owing to the nature of the roads halts are likely to be at irregular times. Coy Commanders will ensure that march

Battalion Orders (contd) 2

discipline is carefully observed. The carrying
of rations in sandbags is forbidden.
8. Breakfast will be at 0500.
9. Kits Officers valises, greatcoats and haversacks
will be dumped in yard of Brewery beside
Bn. Hqrs at 0630
10. A loading party consisting of the pipe band
will parade at Bn. Hqrs. at 0615 to load
G.S. wagons
11. Cookers will be returned to Transport Lines
by 0700
12. Sick parade will be at 0630
13. Lewis Guns (limbers) will be loaded under Company
arrangements by 0700
14. Cookers will be ready for cooking but fires
will not be lighted until orders are given.
15. Water carts will be filled and water bottles
will be full when the march begins.
Bottles to be filled at Brewery at 0530.

Sgt Donaldson
Lcp/Cpl
5/7 Camerons

Operation Order.   Copy No _____

Major [?] Trotter.
Comdg. 1/7th Cameronians (S.R.)

MAP. 20,000 Sheet 45 NW.   10th Nov 1918.

1. **Situation.** Operation resumed, work evident no enemy
W of MONS except a few snipers in BOIS DE BAUDOUR.
   107 Inf Bde are approximately in line with us on
our right, but 75th Inf Bde are some 5 miles behind
on our left.

2. **Intention.** 52nd Div. is continuing its advance eastwards
today.   106 Inf Bde will advance today [?] by
an advance guard under command of Major J.H. SLATER.
1st Royal Scots.

3. **Boundaries.** The N. & S. Bde Boundaries for troop advance will
be
   Northern. an E and W. line through I 6 central.
   Southern. an E and W. line through I 24 central.

4. **Order of March.** The Bn. will pass the starting point
Bridge at I 9 b 0 6. at 07-55. in the following order
   Bn HQ, A, B, C, D, Coys.

5. **Transport.** w.I limbers will move with Coys. Magazine
limber, Medical Cart and one S.A.A. Cart with Bn HQ.
Remainder of transport (Lt. B.Nicholson) will move in rear of the Bn.
to Bde starting point, where it will come under of
B.T.O. (Bde starting point I 15 c 8.9.)

6. **Breakfast** 06-00. Wash Parade 06-45. Officers kits will
be dumped at QM Stores by 07-00.

7. **Water bottles.** R.M. will arrange to fill water bottles
by 07-00

Operation Orders No X

Lieut. Col. J.S.P. Romans D.S.O.
Comdg. 1/7th Bn. The Cameronians (Sco. Rifles).

Ref. Map - TOURNAI 1/100,000.   26th November 1918.

1. Advance party as detailed will proceed to LENS tomorrow to prepare billets for the Battalion which will move there on 28th inst.

2. One Officer and ten men per Coy. i.e. 2 per platoon and 2 per Coy. H.Q.
   Scout Section under L/Cpl. Douglas, Signal Section.
   One representative from the Q.M. Store.

3. The party will parade at the Church, HERCHIES, at 1400 under Lieut. B. Shearer, Lt. 'A' Coy. 2 tool wagons, 2 limbers S.A.A. and 2 limbers from the Q.M. Store, under an N.C.O. to be detailed by Transport Officer, will report to Lieut. Shearer at starting point at 1400 and will accompany party.

4. Each Coy. party will bring one dixie which will be placed in limber at the starting point. The Q.M. will arrange to issue the party's rations in bulk. These will be taken by the party on the limber or sent on later in the Maltese Cart.

5. Cpl. Mitchell, Signal Section, will report to C.O. at 1330 at the crossroads, LENS, in R.6.7.7.

6. Transport Officer will detail limber to collect the party's blankets from Coy. H.Q. and Scout Sections billets, and to join the column by 1400.

7. Road to be followed by the column will be the main HERCHIES - LENS road.

8. Dress - Marching Order - Steel Helmets and Gas Helmets will be carried.

9. Water bottles will be filled before starting.

10. Limbers will return to HERCHIES on completion of duty.

11. Lieut. Shearer will report to Adjutant at 1130 for full instructions.

                                          R.L. Scott Capt. a/Adjt.
                                          1/7th Cameronians (Sco. Rifles).

Operation Order No. V.
by
Lieut Col. J. G. R. Romans, D.S.O.
Comdg. 1/7th Cameronians (Scottish Rifles).

28th Novem., 1918.

1. March to LENS 1315. Order of march, A, C, D, B, & Bn. H.Q. Head of column to pass the Church, HERCHIES, at 1315.
2. Route. HERCHIES – LENS road.
3. Dress. Full Marching Order, jerkins in the pack.
4. Blankets, Officers kits, etc. One G.S. wagon is reporting now to each Coy. including Battn. H.Q. These will be used for blankets, officers kits, etc., and will be loaded as soon as convenient. They will marshall under the Transport Officer at the Church, HERCHIES, at 1200. Lewis Gun wagons will accompany these G.S. wagons and the whole will march under an N.C.O. detailed by Transport Officer.
5. Area vacated will be left scrupulously clean.
6. Sanitation. The M.O. will arrange for the sanitary section to have all latrines filled in by 1245. Pioneer Sergeant will then collect latrine seats and take them to new area. The M.O. will render a report as to the condition these latrines are left in, to reach this office by 1800 tonight.
7. O.C. Coys. will fill up their G.S. wagons with any spare ex-Boche beds (one extra G.S. wagon has been allotted to 'A' Coy. for this purpose).
8. O.C. 'D' Coy. will detail a platoon, under an Officer, as rear party. They will ensure area is left in proper state and will follow the Battalion at 1330.

Copy No. 1. – Lt. 'A' Coy.   No. 5. – Q.M.
       2. –   " B "   6. – T.O.
       3. –   " C "   7. } War Diary.
       4. –   " D "   8. }

D. A. Nelson
Capt. & Adjt.
1/7th Cameronians (S.R.)

Army Form C. 2118.

WAR DIARY
or
INTELLIGENCE SUMMARY.

(Erase heading not required.)

Confidential

Original

A.D.9

War Diary
H.Q. The Cameronians (Scottish Rifles)
December 1918

Volume XLIII

Army Form C. 2118.

WAR DIARY
or
INTELLIGENCE SUMMARY.
(Erase heading not required.)

Instructions regarding War Diaries and Intelligence Summaries are contained in F.S. Regs., Part II. and the Staff Manual respectively. Title pages will be prepared in manuscript.

Adjutant
TOURNAI
1/100000
A1.

Place	Date	Hour	Summary of Events and Information	Remarks and references to Appendices
LENS	DEC 1	1030	Divine Service in School. B Coy billet	Mc
	2		Training Parades 0830 – 1130	Mc
	3		do	Mc
	4		do	Mc
	5		do	Mc
	6		do	Mc
	7		do	Mc
	8			Mc
	9	1015	Divine Service in School	
			Training Parades 0830 – 1130. Commanding officer attended Divisional Conference regarding Education. Leave for men to MONS. Proposed visit to Battlefields of WATERLOO and Sports.	Mc
	10		Training Parades 0830 – 11 30.	Mc
	11		do	Mc
	12		Route march	Mc
	13		Training Parades 0830 – 1130	Mc
	14		do	
	15	1015	Divine Service in School.	Mc
	16		0830 –1000 Educational training 1030 – 1130 Military training.	Mc
	17		0830 – 0930 do 1015 – 1230 Route march.	Mc
	18		0830 – 1000 do 1030 – 1130 Military training	Mc
	19		0830 – 1000 do 1030 – 1130 do	Mc
	20		0830 – 1000 do 1030 – 1130 do	Mc
	21		0830 – 0930 do 1015 – 1230 Route march	Mc
	22	1015	Divine Service in Cinema Hall	Mc
	23		0830 – 1000 Educational training 1030 – 1130 Military training	Mc
	24		0830 – 1000 do 1030 – 1130 do	Mc

War Diary
TOURNAI 1/100000

Army Form C. 2118.

WAR DIARY
or
INTELLIGENCE SUMMARY.
(Erase heading not required.)

Place	Date	Hour	Summary of Events and Information	Remarks and references to Appendices
LENS	DEC 25		Christmas Day: Holiday. Sports. Concert & Dance.	
	26	1015 – 1130	Rudi Mant.	
	27	0830 – 1000	Shoutmas Training 1030 – 1130 Musketry Training	
	28	0830 – 1000	do 1030 – 1130 do	
	29		Church service in D Coy hall. Jocks from Mainet.	
	30	0830 – 1030	Educational Training 1100 – 1200 Military training	
	31	0830 – 1030	do 1100 – 1200 do	

During this month the Education Scheme was started and has proved itself a success. Upon 300 men attend classes daily. Great improvements were made in billets and dining halls for the men through the battalion dining enabled work in making huts, talks, games, athletics benches &c. Demobilization started on 30th the first commenced leaving on that date.

R.M. Blair Major
Commanding 1/7th Cameronians

Strength in the field 30/11/18   26   O.R.
              do   31/12/18   21   584
                                        ───
                                   5 Decrease   692
                                        106 Increase

Officers

Increase
Lt Wordsmith from course
2nd Lt Y. Anderson from leave
2nd Lt G. Brooks   "
2nd Lt G.A. Bentz   "
2nd Lt L.D. Watson "
Capt Nicol A.L. Joined

Decrease
Lt Col G.S.L. Ramsay To Brigade
    Capt Mather as T/Lt Col
  " Muir A.L.
  " Nelson Bn To Leave
  Lt Forbes "
  " Reid   A.L.
  Lt McWilliam D   To TMB
  Lt Smyth   A.L.   To K.O.S.B.
  " Smith   A   "   "
  2nd Lt Stopford   to course
  " Eldred   "

Increase
                O.R.
Reinforcement   1
from Hosp.
Sick   4
Other Causes 1   91
              6   11
                  ───
                  29 st

Decrease
To Hospital   69
Sickness   16
Leave   18
Other Causes   13
              ───
              116

11

A. Wark
Major 7 S.R.
31/12/18.

WAR DIARY
or
INTELLIGENCE SUMMARY.

Army Form C. 2118.

War Diary

7th Bn The Cameronians (Scottish Rifles)

January 1919

Army Form C. 2118.

WAR DIARY
or
INTELLIGENCE SUMMARY.
(Erase heading not required.)

Page 1

Place	Date 1918	Hour	Summary of Events and Information	Remarks and references to Appendices
LENS	Jan 1		New Years Day. Sports. Dance	Attd.
	2	10.15 – 12.00	Route march. Lens – Jurbise, Vivier Roland	Attd.
	3	08.30 – 10.00	Educational training 10.30 – 11.30 military training	Attd.
	4	08.30 – 10.00	do	Attd.
	5	10.00	Divine Service in D Coy Hall	Attd.
	6	08.30 – 10.15	Two Coys on educational training 10.30 – 12.15 two Coys on military training*	Attd.
	7	09.30	Brigade ceremonial march in V2uA	Attd.
	8	08.30 – 10.15 a.m. 10.30 – 12.15	Coys on educational training & military training	Attd.
	9		do	Attd.
	10		do	Attd.
	11		do	Attd.
	12	11.00	Divine Service in B Coy Billet	Attd.
	13	08.30 – 10.15 + 10.30 – 12.15	Educational Training, two Coys at Div Bath LENS.	Attd.
	14		– Do –	Attd.
	15	08.30 – 10.15 a.m 10.30 – 12.15	Educational & Military Training	Attd.
	16		– Do –	Attd.

*There are military trained.

Army Form C. 2118.

WAR DIARY
or
INTELLIGENCE SUMMARY.
(Erase heading not required.)

Page 2

Place	Date	Hour	Summary of Events and Information	Remarks and references to Appendices
LENS	1918 Jan 17	09.20	Practice Parade for Divisional Ceremonial Parade, held in 1/4 Royal Scots Parade Ground	Orders
	18	07.15	Battn moved off to Divisional Parade in K.9.d.10	Orders
	19	10.15	Church Service in D Coy Hall	Orders
	20	08.30-10.15 a.m 10.30-12.15	Coys Educational musketry training	Orders
	21		Do	Orders
	22		Do	Orders
	23	08.30-10.15 a.m 10.30-12.15	Coys Educational training musketry	Orders
	24		Coys Educational Musketry training	Orders
	25		Do	Orders
	26	10.50	Church Service in Cinema Hall	Orders
	27	08.30-10.15 a.m 10.30-12.15	Coys Educational training musketry training	Orders
	28		Do	Orders
	29		Coys Educational training musketry	Orders
	30		Do	Orders
	31		Coys Educational musketry training	Orders

Army Form C. 2118.

WAR DIARY
or
INTELLIGENCE SUMMARY.
(Erase heading not required.)

Page 3

Place	Date	Hour	Summary of Events and Information	Remarks and references to Appendices
			During the month January 11th to 31st 150 O.R. was demobilized and the numbers attending Educational Classes were reduced considerably. A Lecturer Cinema was inaugurated 24/1/19 and proved a great success. Towards the end of the month however new programmes are difficult to obtain. May improvements in the billets were effected. Recreation rooms were widened, and lighting was considerably improved. Robert Blair Lt Col	

WAR DIARY
or
INTELLIGENCE SUMMARY

Army Form C. 2118.

War Diary

1/5th Cameronians (Scottish Rifles)

March 1919

Army Form C. 2118.

WAR DIARY
or
INTELLIGENCE SUMMARY.
(Erase heading not required.)

Instructions regarding War Diaries and Intelligence Summaries are contained in F. S. Regs., Part II. and the Staff Manual respectively. Title pages will be prepared in manuscript.

Place	Date	Hour	Summary of Events and Information	Remarks and references to Appendices
Lens Belgium	1/3/19		"Summer Time" came into force. All available men on P.T/a.	
	2/3/19		Trg. Divy. Lectures on Mexico	
	3/3/19		Bathing. All available men on P.T/a. Padre Claremont to Hopiten sick.	
	4/3/19		Holiday – 56th Division Race meeting MAZIERRE	
	5/3/19		All available men on Guard duty and Lewis Guns	
	6/3/19		Do.	
	7/3/19		Do.	
	8/3/19		Do.	
	9/3/19		Do.	
	10/3/19		Bathing.	
	11/3/19		All available men on Guard Duty and Lewis Guns	
	12/3/19		Do.	
	13/3/19		Do.	
	14/3/19		Medical Inspection of unit. Do.	
	15/3/19		All available men on Guard Duty and L.G/a.	
	16/3/19		Lt. Col. R.R.Blair proceeded to U.K. Do.	

Army Form C. 2118.

WAR DIARY
or
INTELLIGENCE SUMMARY.
(Erase heading not required.)

Instructions regarding War Diaries and Intelligence Summaries are contained in F. S. Regs., Part II. and the Staff Manual respectively. Title pages will be prepared in manuscript.

Place	Date	Hour	Summary of Events and Information	Remarks and references to Appendices
Sone Belgium	17/3/19			
Soignies	18/3/19		Battalion moved to SOIGNIES by march route.	
	19/3/19		All available men on fg's and packing stoves for impending move of Battalion	
	20/3/19		Do	Do
	21/3/19		Do	Do
	22/3/19		Do	Do
	23/3/19		Do	Do Lt. A.T. Collet to U.K.
	24/3/19		Do	Do 2/Lt W.T.Anderson Struck off strength
	25/3/19		Do	Do
	26/3/19		Do	Do
	27/3/19		Do	Do
	28/3/19		Inspection of Stores by D.A.D.O.S.	
	29/3/19		All available men on General Fatigue	
	30/3/19		Do	Do
	31/3/19		Do	Do

Since the month 38 men were demobilized, bringing the Regiment down to Cadre strength. During the second part of the month all men were employed on various Orders Policies, and trainings, preparing for the Battalion proceeding from Soignies to mores to SOIGNIE S, the troops of the Nation are being treated by the Civilians and militarily — Youth Concerts themes then to Officers and early Cinemas etc.

Strength in the field 31/12/18   O.   O.R.
                      do. 31/1/19   21   692
                                     ___ ___
                                      19   841
                                     2 Decrease 151 Decrease

Increase	O.	O.R.
Reinforcements		
From home		53
From base	4	14
Other causes	3	4
	7	91

Decrease		
Invalided	4	156
To Hospital	1	40
On leave	1	9
Other causes	3	27
	9	232

Increase.

Capt Wilson from leave
Lt B.S. Forbes   "   "
Lt J. McWilliam   "   "
Capt Phillips   "   "
2Lt Crystal ?   " course
2Lt Nicholson   "   "
2Lt H. Smith   "   "

Decrease.

Lt Hopkins to Sea
Capt Boniface Absent
Lt Henderson
2Lt Gourlie   "
2Lt Reid   "
Capt Arthur to ? Army
Lt Collie to hospital
2Lt Lindsay to base
2Lt D. Callen to ?

D. McWilliam Lt/Acct Adjt
for OC 1/4 Lt Cameronians
(Sco Rifles)

www.ingramcontent.com/pod-product-compliance
Lightning Source LLC
Chambersburg PA
CBHW081407160426
43193CB00013B/2125